Helion & Company Limited
Unit 8 Amherst Business Centre
Budbrooke Road
Warwick
CV34 5WE
England
Tel. 01926 499 619
Email: info@helion.co.uk
Website: www.helion.co.uk
Twitter: @helionbooks
https://helionbooks.wordpress.com/

Cover: M-1978 Koksan SPGs firing during an exercise. (KCBC)

Designed and typeset by Mach 3 Solutions (www.mach3solutions.co.uk)
Cover design Paul Hewitt, Battlefield Design (www.battlefield-design.co.uk)

ISBN: 978-1-804519-66-0

British Library Cataloguing-in-Publication Data
A catalogue record for this book is available from the British Library

CONTENTS

(Map by George Anderson)

ABBREVIATIONS AND ACRONYMNS

AA	anti-air
AFV	armoured fighting vehicle
AGL	automatic grenade launcher
APC	armoured personnel carrier
APS	active protection system
ARV	armoured recovery vehicle
ATGM	anti-tank guided missile
CEP	circular error probable
C4ISR	command, control, communications, computers, intelligence, surveillance and reconnaissance
DMZ	Demilitarized Zone
DoD	Department of Defense (US)
DPRK	Democratic People's Republic of Korea
ERA	explosive reactive armour
GLATGM	gun-launched anti-tank guided missile
GNSS	global navigation satellite system
GPS	Global Positioning System
FCS	fire control system
HE	high explosive
HEAT	high explosive anti-tank warhead
IADS	integrated air defence system
IR	infrared
KCBC	Korean Central Broadcasting Committee
KCNA	Korean Central News Agency
KPA	Korean People's Army
KPAAF	Korean People's Army Air and Anti-Air Force
KPAGF	Korean People's Army Ground Force
LRF	laser rangefinder
LWR	laser warning receiver
MANPADS	man-portable air-defence system
MBT	main battle tank
MRL	multiple rocket launcher
NBC	nuclear, biological, chemical
RAP	rocket-assisted projectile
RHA	rolled homogeneous armour
ROK	Republic of Korea [South]
ROKA	Republic of Korea Army [South]
SAM	surface-to-air missile
SEAD	suppression of enemy air defences
SHORAD	short range air defence
SPAAG	self-propelled anti-aircraft gun
SPG	self-propelled gun
SPM	self-propelled mortar
UN	United Nations
US	United States
USA	United States of America

INTRODUCTION

Infantry, and the tactics shaping their use, will play a central role in any future conflict on the Korean Peninsula, alongside the APCs and fire-support vehicles detailed in the previous volume. However, it is through the overwhelming firepower of its armoured formations and artillery, backed by engineering units and mobile air defences, that the KPA is expected to attempt a breakthrough. With most of its inventory of indigenous manufacture, the present book attempts a comprehensive study into the little-explored landscape of the Ground Forces' armoured fighting vehicles.

1

TANKS

With its narrow corridors and high concentrations of forces, the areas around the Demilitarized Zone (DMZ) are liable to become the scene of one of the largest tank battles in history should fighting erupt; the Korean People's Army (KPA) fields some 4,300 tanks, facing off roughly 2,200 more of the Republic of Korea Army (ROKA). Nonetheless, much of the Korean Peninsula is relatively inhospitable to main battle tanks (MBTs), with engagement ranges marred by a plethora of mountain ranges covered in dense forest. The preciously rare flats are riddled with rivers that can become obstacles that are hard to overcome should their bridges be dismantled and have in the South often been seized by eager urbanisation. To an invasive force then, highly mobile, lightweight and preferably amphibious, or at least fording-capable, tank designs that are optimised for short-range engagements are preferable. Although these requirements have been strictly adhered to in the KPA, with tanks usually weighing below 40 tonnes, as opposed to the 55 tonnes of South Korea's K2, there is a huge qualitative difference on average between the North's current tank composition and that of the South. Against the ROKA's crème de la crème the KPA has little to offer in terms of MBTs, with only a few dozen of its most capable designs currently thought to be in service. As such it will likely aim to use its tank force as a force multiplier for its mechanised forces rather than instigating direct tank-on-tank engagements, and leave hard targets such as the K2 to dedicated anti-tank teams. Still, the 105th Tank Division remains one of the most esteemed units in the KPA, and its tank units will form the sharp edge of the spearhead into the South if an invasion is mounted.

How its vast armour forces and current tank composition came to be is the result of a long and quite unconventional process, one dating all the way back to the establishment of the first tank unit in 1948. After the successes gained using Soviet-legacy tanks such as the T-34 during the Korean War, North Korea adhered to a tank procurement programme unique for a nation of its size and economic means. Its modern inventory still has its foundations in the vast numbers of T-54s, Type-59s and T-55s acquired and produced after the Korean War (the venerable IS-2 and ISU-122, available only in small numbers, have been retired), which was expanded once again by large numbers of indigenously manufactured T-62s in the 1970s and 80s. Although it has since moved on to producing large numbers of indigenously designed tanks based on both aforementioned types as well as the T-72, it remains the sole nation to base the bulk of its tank forces around the T-62 today. Aside from these MBTs it also operates numerous amphibious and light tanks, originally centred around Soviet-delivered PT-76Bs and Chinese Type-62 and Type-63 tanks but nowadays including an indigenous offspring designated the Sinhung. While the majority of this roughly 4,300-strong force is by modern standards extremely outdated, it is its indigenous industry that has introduced a measure of uncertainty in its capabilities. Even though the bulk of its forces function mainly as light armour, well suited to navigating the mountainous and river-crossed landscape of the Korean Peninsula, its newest designs also have some chance of facing off against South Korean designs such as the K1 and K2 tank families.

Soon after the Korean War the Democratic People's Republic of Korea (DPRK) already set out to modify its tank force to better allow it to cope with threats encountered on the battlefield. These constitute some of its first efforts towards indigenously enhancing the effectiveness of its fighting vehicles and make North Korea a particularly early adopter of slat armour. Both T-34/76s and T-34/85s in KPA service have been overhauled, the latter sporting snorkels, T-55-pattern 'starfish' road wheels, new sprockets, tracks, attachments for slat armour and possibly new communications equipment. These upgrades have allowed some examples to remain in KPA reserves to this day, a good example of North Korean reluctance to retire anything before it is properly irreparable.

Mere overhauls of older equipment are insufficient if one desires to remain competitive internationally however, and from an early stage North Korea emphasised the importance of setting up an indigenous arms industry to enable it to independently arm its forces regardless of which way the political wind was blowing. Although its post-war MBT force, mainly consisting of roughly 1,000 T-34s and as few as 12 IS-2s, was at first supplemented by small numbers of T-54-3s, which immediately entered service with the 105th Tank Division, during the 1950s, a true replacement of this legacy armour would take until the turmoil of the 1960s.

A T-34/76 charges forward with infantry riding on top in a training exercise. (KCBC)

During this period the deliveries of PT-76B amphibious light tanks and T-55 MBTs were promptly paired with the founding of an indigenous tank industry, which according to North Korean sources churned out its first copy of the PT-76B in 1967 and of the T-54A in 1968.[1] Although these dates are unlikely to refer to the start of serial production, or presumably assembly in the case of the PT-76B, which actually commenced in the early 1970s, it is likely factories such as the Sinhung and Kusong tank plant were indeed set up or retooled for these designs in this period with Soviet aid.[2] Interestingly, these indigenously produced T-54As were fitted with a 14.5mm KPV instead of the more common 12.7mm DShK. The KPV heavy machine gun has been highly favoured in the DPRK since the early stages of the Cold War and has since remained popular as a light anti-aircraft (AA) and ground support weapon. Today it functions mainly as a deterrent against Republic of Korea Air Force and US Air Force helicopters and slow-flying aircraft. In practice, the weapon is cumbersome to use, and when mounted on the T-54/55 a special attachment point to the rear of the turret is used to ensure stability during travel. That the fledgling tank industry could not yet satisfy all the KPA's armour needs at this point is attested by the acquisition of large numbers of Type-59s alongside T-55s in the mid to late 1960s and the 1970s. The former of these two do sport the 12.7mm DShK on their turret, and the fact that many are now fitted with the 14.5mm KPV instead seems to indicate that the KPV was valued enough that they were at some point modified for its use.

The DPRK has exploited any opportunity to upgrade its T-34/85s so they retain some combat relevance. This has included the installation of slat armour, new road wheels and tracks but also a snorkel (not visible here) to allow the tank to cross rivers by driving across the riverbed. While one might quickly predict the outcome of direct engagements between T-34s and opposing M1 Abrams' or K2s along the DMZ, its relevance should be sought as part of a rear echelon following the main advance or for rear area defence in the DPRK. (Artwork by David Bocquelet)

A North Korean T-54A or Type-59 with a KPV attached to the rear of the turret. (KCBC)

The next project, of a much more ambitious calibre, would result in a technological advantage over the South that would last for almost a decade. The exact origins of the North Korean programme that would see its tank forces transformed until they were centred around the Soviet T-62 are unclear, and several specifics remain to be answered. Two competing theories suggest either Soviet-sanctioned licence production and the delivery of entire production lines in the early to mid 1970s, or the exact opposite in the form of a reverse engineering effort some years later.[3] Even a conflation of both theories, with Soviets delivering an initial production capacity but later retracting aid after relations turned sour in the mid 1970s, remains a possibility. What is known is that by the late 1970s production of T-54s slowly dwindled while factories were retooled for producing the T-62, in which they apparently first succeeded in 1976 under the indigenous designation of Chonma.[4] No T-62s were ever acquired in any substantial numbers from abroad, and the fact that the North Korean variant featured a range of indigenous design elements casts doubt on the delivery of an initial production capacity in the form of components. Curiously, the main design of the Chonma was borrowed from both the T-62 Obr. 1962 and the Obr. 1972, sharing its chassis with the former but utilising the turret of the latter. Its turret was further modified to allow for the mounting of a 14.5mm KPV, necessitating a redesign of the handrails so spares of its large 14.5x114mm magazines could be fitted. Series production of the Chonma began in 1978, with the tanks entering armoured divisions in earnest numbers during the 1980s, earning the US DoD (Department of Defense) moniker of T-628.[5] Large scale exports of this iconic North Korean tank began during the same period, with some 150 Chonmas exported to Iran between 1982 and 1985 during the Iran-Iraq War, and smaller numbers to Ethiopia.[6] While Ethiopia's stock of Chonmas appears to have been completely exhausted during the 1980s and 1990s, a limited number of Iranian examples are still kept in service, and one even fell into the hands of US forces during the 2003 invasion of Iraq (where it had ended up after the Iran-Iraq War). Another present-day user is Eritrea, which likely inherited a number of these MBTs from Ethiopia after the Eritrean War of Independence. Since procurement from the Soviet Union was no longer an option, the indigenous production of tanks was for this period the only way of providing

One of the North Korean Chonma tanks exported to Iran in the 1980s. This particular example was captured by Iraq during the Iran-Iraq War and later recovered by US forces in 2003. (Till Sunderman)

A Chonma sits destroyed outside the Ethiopian Presidential Palace in Addis Ababa after a battle between government forces and rebels in 1991. (Ed Boyce, US DoD)

at least somewhat modern equipment for the KPA, aside from the Type-59s offered by the Chinese. As a result, tanks common to many other nations that were aligned with the Soviet Union such as the T-55A or more advanced variants of the T-55 and T-62 were never delivered. Nonetheless, producing tanks indigenously and possibly without licence was a remarkable achievement, and no other states under Soviet influence had set up production lines for the T-62 MBT, with only Czechoslovakia and Poland producing the T-54/55 series at the time.[7] By comparison, South Korea had only just received early variants of the M48 Patton to supplement the even more outdated M47 Patton, both still armed with a 90mm cannon. These tanks were obviously no match for the T-62's smoothbore 115mm U-5TS cannon, a technological marvel at the time of its introduction. In other areas the T-62's performance was less impressive however, and it is – not without justification – often regarded as little more capable than the T-55, as both are similarly marred by poor accuracy and relatively ineffective munitions.

While the Chonma MBT line would later know extensive additions and upgrades to enhance its capabilities and mitigate its shortcomings, the next indigenous development came in the form of the Sinhung amphibious light tank, also known by the US DoD as the M-1985, introduced in 1981. This tank is often incorrectly described as using an armoured personnel carrier (APC) chassis with an up-gunned PT-76 turret. However, although incorporating features from both the Soviet PT-76B and the Chinese Type 63, it can certainly be called the first truly North Korean designed tank as almost all of its major components differ significantly from their ancestors. It came with an indigenously designed 85mm rifled cannon reminiscent of the 85mm Type 62-85TC used by the Chinese Type 62 and Type 63, which had been delivered in the 1970s, and used a chassis later shared by the Chunma-D APC. It weighs 20 tonnes, can reach a top speed of 60 kilometres per hour on land and 10 kilometres per hour in the water, to a maximum operational range of 500 kilometres, according to North Korean sources.[8] Perhaps due to its similarity to the PT-76 and because of either the date it was first spotted (1985) or the calibre of its cannon (85mm), this vehicle is sometimes also referred to as the PT-85, even though this designation is used neither by North Korea itself nor the US DoD. While the Sinhung was seen carrying a Malyutka anti-tank guided missile (ATGM) over its main gun in the parade for the 40th anniversary of the Fatherland Liberation War in 1985, this feature had been removed from the new variant spotted in the parade for the 60th anniversary of the Korean People's Army in 1992, which also incorporates a slightly redesigned turret outfitted with an IR searchlight and accompanying night vision optic. Whether the ATGM was actually compatible with the vehicle or if it was just added for disinformation purposes is unknown, although the latter appears to be most likely. In recent years, the Sinhung has also been refitted with three smoke grenade dischargers on either side of its turret as part of a programme that seeks to enhance the survivability of a whole range of KPA vehicles in this fashion.

Other, much more obscure amphibious tank designs have also enjoyed modest production runs but are nowadays far less widely deployed if at all. One such example thought to originate from the late 1970s or early 1980s is a 323-based light amphibious tank utilising a turret with a close resemblance to that of the PT-76B, and a different 85mm main cannon patterned after the Chinese Type 62-85TC. The rear door was removed and the PT-76B's waterjets are also fitted, thus in effect recreating much of the Sinhung's characteristics – indicating that it may in fact have preceded its development. While the Soviet PT-76B is to North Korea the origin of the amphibious tank concept, it is unsurprising that in the DPRK such vehicles have been invested in especially aggressively. Given the myriad of rivers complicating operations in the South, much of the KPA's mechanised forces have been geared towards amphibious operations. This includes APCs, troop carriers, light air defence and artillery support; heavy armour is generally limited to fording, which is not applicable to larger or wilder rivers.[9] For larger river crossings, either bridges, ferries or pontoon bridges will be required, which take precious time to set up and are under threat of aerial bombardment. As such, the amphibious tank fulfils a unique role in providing fire support to units swiftly advancing through landscapes with many rivers running through them. Of course, sacrificing heavy armour for their amphibious capabilities, they do not stand a chance against enemy MBTs or anti-tank weaponry, and require careful use to exploit their full potential.

Sinhung light tanks pass rows of spectators in Pyongyang during the 100th anniversary of Kim Il Sung's birthday parade in 2012. Later examples would be fitted with 2x3 smoke grenade dischargers on either side of the turret. (David Flack)

Subsequent developments in the Chonma line progressed through the addition of various types of laser range finders (LRFs), new variants of which are being developed to this day. Curiously enough, even though the LRFs can be mounted on several vehicles in service with the Korean People's Army, they are rarely seen on older generation North Korean tanks. However, many of these LRFs were produced for export, resulting in a part of the Syrian T-54/55 fleet being equipped with North Korean LRFs – some even with 14.5mm KPV heavy machineguns – wind sensors and accompanying fire control systems (FCS) in the late 1970s or early 1980s. These upgraded examples saw action in the 1982 Lebanon War and in the Syrian Civil War. Curiously, none of the factions involved in the Syrian Civil War appear to have actually made use of the LRF, possibly because it is difficult to operate or requires frequent maintenance. Nonetheless, such devices could drastically increase the accuracy of older generations of KPA tanks, which is especially of use when trying to land a hit with the first shot – a feat which most modern MBTs effortlessly pull off. However, costs likely prohibited a wider introduction of this technology to the KPA, and most older tanks still do entirely without.

Following the introduction of tanks equipped with LRFs, little imagery or information is available from North Korean sources until the early 1990s. However, several intriguing designs have been spotted in this period. Even though the first of these designs is spotted only rarely, it was a clear indication of the progress of North Korea's tank industry. Improvements came in the form of a redesigned turret, replacing the original T-62 Obr. 1972's turret seen on the early-generation Chonmas. The revamped turret featured an extended rear section, likely housing additional ammunition –

Rarely sighted yet confirmed to be in operational service with the KPA is this 323-based light amphibious tank. Presumably part of a short production run as an interim vehicle prior to the introduction of the superior Sinhung tank, the tank nonetheless typifies the North Korean tank concept of highly mobile, lightweight and amphibious designs optimised for short-range engagements. (Artwork by David Bocquelet)

a feature thought to have been retained on other Chonma variants since. The T-62's hull munition racks are only accessible while the turret is facing forward, so that additional readily available rounds in the turret are likely much appreciated. The turret was also fitted with attachment points allowing for the use of slat armour, which helps defeat incoming anti-tank rockets by disrupting their shaped charge. A cheap alternative to more cumbersome unconventional armour upgrades, North Korea was one of the first nations in the world to employ slat armour on a large scale. Provision for slat armour was later installed on nearly all of Pyongyang's T-34/85s, T-54/55s, Type-59s and early Chonmas, although it is rarely seen mounted during exercises. Even though this early upgraded Chonma variant is confirmed to be in service, its relative rarity in propaganda footage makes it unlikely it was produced in very large numbers. Despite the fact that this tank represented a step forward in the DPRK's tank industry, no LRF was present, and aside from the optional slat armour no other protection enhancements are apparent. However, in the parade for the 40th anniversary of the Fatherland Liberation War in 1985 a new LRF was spotted on a Chonma, which subsequently received the designation of 'Chonma-ho II' by the US DoD. This LRF-equipped tank preluded the commencement of the production of a new generation of Chonmas which would see far more radical modifications and upgrades introduced at a faster pace than achieved before.

A Syrian T-55 with upgraded North Korean FCS narrowly being missed by an ATGM. Note the bulky LRF atop the main gun, which does not appear to have entered active service in the DPRK itself. (Authors' archive)

Kim Jong Il next to a T-55 fitted with slat armour. Although most tanks in KPA service are capable of donning this extra layer of protection, they are rarely spotted actually doing so. (KCBC)

A Chonma MBT with an extended turret for additional ammunition stowage. (KCBC)

Kim Jong Il inspects a Chonma MBT fitted with an LRF over its main gun. This type does not appear to have entered service in North Korea. (KCBC)

Having successfully achieved production of the T-62 and even embarked on various modest programmes to upgrade the type, North Korea at the end of the 1980s began looking ahead to the next generation of MBTs. The obvious choice at the time seemed like the T-72, which was prolifically entering service with a range of nations aligned with the Soviet Union. Tellingly, the CIA predicted in 1987 that T-62 production would swiftly taper off in favour of the T-72 during the 1990s.[10] And indeed, the fact that North Korea was eyeing the introduction of technologies found in the T-72 cannot be denied, given subsequent developments. Where they sourced this technology from has long remained a mystery, however. What is known is that North Korea managed to procure a single battle-damaged T-72 'Ural' in the early or mid 1980s from Iran, which had captured it from Iraq during the Iran-Iraq War. By 1985, a legitimate path opened up that did not require lengthy reverse engineering as relations with the Soviet Union mended. An actual purchase might not have been realistic given the North's interests in developing its indigenous armour industry (and the nations' deteriorating finances), but Russian sources do report that licensed production

The sole publicly existing image of North Korea's T-72 'Ural' during an inspection by Kim Il Sung and Kim Jong Il in the mid 1980s. (KCBC)

'M-1992' MBTs drive past North Korean schoolchildren in Pyongyang during the 1992 parade commemorating the 60th anniversary of the Korean People's Army. (KCBC)

of T-72Ms was authorised in 1988 with production to be set up in 1991.[11, 12] This move might well have been in response to South Korea's unveiling of their K1 MBT that same year. Production of the T-72 ultimately did not materialise however.

Instead, the early 1990s saw the development of a series of closely related MBTs based on the Chonma but incorporating new technologies possibly derived from the T-72. The first publicly known product of this second generation of Chonmas was spotted during the 1992 parade commemorating the 60th anniversary of the Korean People's Army, which is most often linked to the US DoD designations of 'M-1992', 'Chonma-ho III' and occasionally 'T-668'. It sported an ambitious series of innovations, including what appears to be a modified hull sporting composite armour in the glacis, side skirts (the quality of which differs between field and parade units), and a rearranged engine deck reflective of a switch to the T-72's V-46 engine. The most striking difference with earlier Chonmas is seemingly unrelated to Soviet tanks however, consisting of the angular outlay of the turret armour, giving the turret a much more modern look. It is believed this is the result of a switch in production from traditional cast turrets to welded ones, which are simpler to make and allow for more advanced armour compositions.[13] The turret also incorporates advances in the area of LRF technology, as well as sporting modest amounts of explosive reactive armour (ERA) and two rows of four smoke grenade dischargers on either side, both of which were new to the KPA at the time. Curiously, some examples were seen outfitted with an apparent additional IR searchlight next to the L-2 and FG-100/125 set, similar in appearance to the commander's OU-3. There is no conceivable utility to this addition, and it was only observed once. The weight of the tank is believed to have been increased from the T-62's 37 tonnes to 38 tonnes, likely reflecting the upgrades in turret and hull armour.[14] Production seems to have been more than a token effort, with the tanks making sporadic appearances in the field. Moreover, a rare second type has on occasion been spotted that sports a slightly different arrangement of the smoke grenade dischargers and a modified LRF, suggesting development continued.

From North Korean sources a third configuration by the name of Chonma-92 is known that appears to be outfitted with just four smoke grenade dischargers on either side of the turret and a different ERA arrangement, providing far larger coverage of not just the turret but also the hull. Whether the 'M-1992' and this tank received the same designation in North Korean service is unknown. The presence of ERA on these tanks so early in the 1990s is highly remarkable, and considering later incarnations of the Chonma tank line lacked any kind of ERA, it is possible that it was created for the sole purpose of propaganda/disinformation. Nevertheless, it is more likely that North Korea got its hands on an early transfer of ERA technology from the Soviet Union in the brief period of the 1980s that relations were mended and used this on the 'M-1992' and Chonma-92. In similar vein, the tanks are notable for introducing a thermal shroud to the main gun, mirroring developments on the T-62M and T-72 'Ural-1'. This is likely why rumours persist of a mysterious development attributed to this period carrying the US DoD designation of 'Chonma-ho IV or V', which supposedly switched its legacy 115mm U-5TS for a North Korean version of the T-72's 125mm D-81T(M). While it is certainly technically feasible to install this cannon inside a modified T-62 turret due to their comparable dimensions, tanks in this generation seem to preserve the T-62-legacy cannon instead. Development of these types is sometimes also linked with Romania, with which the DPRK upheld strong relations during this period, and which had an expansive tank development programme itself. Romanian cooperation with the DPRK in military fields has indeed left its traces in the KPA's arsenal, yet there are no direct signs of Romanian influence on Pyongyang's tank industry. Wildly divergent reports of T-72M/S, T-80BV or even T-90S acquired in the years hence appear not to have been grounded

Another 'M-1992'-like Chonma with serial 216. This particular example inspected by Kim Jong Il in 2008 has been spotted on multiple occasions, but whether the type was actually produced in meaningful numbers is unknown. (KCBC)

Kim Jong Un walks past an ERA-equipped Chonma-92 during the opening of the KPA Exhibition of Arms and Equipment in Pyongyang in April 2012. (KCBC)

The Chonma-98 at its sole public display at the KPA Exhibition of Arms and Equipment in Pyongyang. (KCBC)

in reality either, and indeed North Korea's current tank technology appears to be based on either the T-62, the T-72 'Ural' acquired in the 1980s or indigenous research. Regardless of whether the reports of an early 125mm-armed tank in the 1990s are correct, subsequent variants of the Chonma retained the 115mm U-5TS cannon.

The next documented progression in the Chonma series was the Chonma-98, which like the Chonma-92 is notable for only ever having been displayed publicly at the KPA Exhibition of Arms and Equipment. Although the '92' part of Chonma-92 may refer to the date of its inception (1992), such a connection between designation and year was discontinued in later production models. The Chonma-98 is an odd example of this, stemming from the year 2000 (or Juche 89).[15] The naming is not the only curious aspect of the tank, as it reverted the hull modernisations of the previous generation to make use of a mostly unmodified T-62 chassis. Moreover, the turret, while left largely identical to the Chonma-92, was stripped of its ERA, and the main gun of its thermal shroud. While it is unknown what prompted this apparent technological backslide, it is possible that the changes reflect the removal of foreign-sourced components that had become increasingly hard to source following the collapse of the Soviet Union and the consequent North Korean economic hardships. This would include the T-72's engine (and associated components like the transmission), ERA, aluminium thermal shroud, and composite armour components. While progress on tank design thus stagnated, there is some evidence that efforts to improve tanker gear persisted during the austerity of the 1990s. In a 1995 incident, a North Korean national was arrested in Russia trying to smuggle military equipment including PNV-57E semi-passive night vision goggles.[16]

The Chonma-98 was succeeded by the Chonma-214 in 2001 (Juche 90), which featured appliqué armour on the front of a remodelled turret and a slightly modified chassis with bolted-on glacis armoured plating and two steel plates on either side of the hull, which was to remain the standard for later Chonmas. However, the tank's weight was not increased, maintaining the Chonma-92/98's 38 tonnes. This was the first tank to be equipped with appliqué armour on the turret with attached rubber flaps, providing the Chonma-214 with an additional estimated 100mm of protection against APDS-type munitions and up to around 200mm of protection against shaped charge and HEAT (high explosive anti-tank) ammunition. While it still made do with the T-62-legacy 115mm main gun, the Chonma-214 was also the first in the series to be visibly influenced by the T-72. Although subtle in nature, the altered front drive wheel, also seen on all later Chonma incarnations, is sufficiently similar to the one seen on the T-72 to draw conclusions on its origin. Given the fact that it had at this point been available for close to two decades, it is highly unlikely that this is the only component that saw influence from the T-72, and less visible modifications

Chonma-214 MBTs. Note the appliqué armour lined with rubber flaps covering its shot trap, a feature not seen on other Chonma iterations. (David Flack)

such as in the FCS are probable. Although North Korea does not have access to the rare metals which can be used to create truly effective modern munitions, the DPRK must produce its own 115mm ammunition and has in all likelihood experimented with more advanced penetrators to increase the lethality of the U-5TS as well.

A Chonma-215 MBT during the 65th anniversary of the Workers' Party of Korea parade in 2010. Note the remodelled appliqué armour, extensive sensor suite and loudspeakers. (KCBC)

The next progression in the Chonma tank tree represents somewhat of an oddball in the midst of other progressively improved Chonma variants. First produced in 2003 (Juche 92), the Chonma-215 is sighted only rarely, and featured solely in the 65th anniversary of the Workers' Party of Korea in 2010. Despite its elusive nature (perhaps resulting in both it and the Chonma-214 being referred to as the 'M-2002' by the US DoD), the Chonma-215 represented several key advancements in the North Korean tank industry. Most notably, the traditional T-62-style chassis with five road wheels was replaced by one that features six road wheels in roughly the same suspension as on the T-62 but with one additional axle. The length of the tank was not appreciably altered, but armour thickness and composition of the glacis was likely altered significantly. It seems many of the T-62's hull features – including the engine screen and presumably the engine – were retained however, and it even still uses the characteristic 'starfish' shaped road wheels also seen on the T-55 and T-62, albeit reduced in size by some 10 percent to match that of the T-72's road wheels. Clearly, the resources required to adopt the T-72's aluminium road wheels was not considered worthwhile. The appliqué armour on the front of the turret was reinforced and the rubber plates were removed. This reinforced appliqué armour fitted the shape of the turret more closely, resulting in the need for the IR searchlight to be moved slightly closer to the LRF. Additional appliqué armour was fitted to the hull front, further increasing the tank's frontal aspect armour values, though leaving considerable gaps in coverage. Other evidence points towards a heavily upgraded FCS, using various sensors – amongst which is a wind sensor. The weight of the vehicle was increased to 39 tonnes, but the presence of additional streamlined fuel tanks atop the right hand tracks suggest its range is unaltered or improved.[17] Interestingly, the Chonma-215 was also equipped with loudspeakers for commandeering infantry fighting alongside the tank, which was to feature subsequent designs as well. This reflects the DPRK's military strategy, in which tanks and infantry are slated to spearhead the offensive alongside each other.

The penultimate development of the Chonma series, combining many technologies found on earlier Chonma tanks with foreign influences, was named the Chonma-216 (US DoD designation 'M-2009'). First produced in 2004 (Juche 93), its name refers to the birth date of Kim Jong Il, 16 February 1941. This date is also reflected in a number of other aforementioned tank designs, all bearing the turret serial number 216. As the previous two models have designations that count up towards 216, it is likely that these were mostly experimental only in nature and as a result produced in limited numbers – possibly just a few dozen of each. Although initially attributed specifically to the Chonma-216, foreign sources have come to ascribe to almost all of North Korea's post-2000 tank ventures the designator 'P'okp'ung-ho', which creates much confusion by blending in different lines of development under a single name. North Korean sources make no mention of such a designation actually being in use, and even outright identify it as entirely incorrect.[18] The Chonma-216 put the experience gained on the Chonma-215 into practice by the introduction of a fully developed chassis with six road wheels, bearing much resemblance to that of the Soviet T-72. The suspension and engine deck were wholly redesigned, copying over many features and an upgraded engine from the T-72, increasing its mobility and reliability. Nonetheless, the position of the driver is still on the left side of the hull, an important reminder that the tank still has its roots in the T-62 as opposed to the T-72, where the driver takes up a central position. In similar fashion, the rear drive sprocket and OMSh metallic hinge tracks of the T-62 found their way into the design of the Chonma-216, and 215 for that matter. The reason for this fact finds its origin in the Kusong tank factory, responsible for building the bulk of the DPRK's tanks and spare parts. As rerolling factory lines for producing T-72 parts such as RMSh tracks would be a heavy burden on the already fragile North Korean logistics system, many of the T-62's original parts are incorporated even on new-production tanks. Due to the high degree of commonality between T-55 and T-62 parts, this means the Kusong tank factory alone is capable of producing spare parts for nearly all MBTs in service in the DPRK. Despite these far-reaching changes, the weight of the tank supposedly remains at 39 tonnes.[19] The turret also saw no major changes compared to the Chonma-215, with only the smoke grenade launchers being rearranged and possibly the use of a new variant of the LRF. Though it remains difficult to estimate characteristics like armour values of modern North Korean MBTs without insider knowledge, the fact that an indigenously designed ATGM (the Bulsae-4M) whose penetration values are known was demonstrated against the Chonma-216 gives us some indication. Multiple thermobaric and armour piercing warheads were used against it during these tests in 2016, with one of the latter shots, which is claimed to be capable of penetrating 700mm RHA, narrowly avoiding the appliqué armour on the turret front but seemingly not penetrating, and another penetrating the turret roof.

During the 2013 parade for the 60th anniversary of the Korean War armistice analysts were given the first hint that new armament packages were being developed for the KPA's most modern tanks, in a highly unconventional move in tank design. The true intent behind this new direction of design was only revealed in imagery from a tank competition and the subsequent parade for the 105th anniversary of Kim Il Sung's birthday in 2017 however. In it, Chonma-216s were showcased that featured weapons systems that represent a major departure from traditional tank building. Most ostentatious were three separate systems replacing the tank's regular secondary armament, comprising a dual ATGM launcher,

Chonma-216 MBTs of the Seoul Ryu Kyong Su Guards 105th Tank Division engage in a firing drill during an exercise in 2024. Note the T-72-style rear and chassis. (KCBC)

a retractable surface-to-air missile (SAM) launcher and a dual automatic grenade launcher (AGL), each automated to allow them to be fired from within the turret. The ATGMs, consisting of the North Korean Bulsae-2 or their upgraded variants, lend the vehicle a long-ranged anti-tank capability that was severely lacking due to its outdated main gun and inability to fire gun-launched anti-tank guided missiles (GLATGMs). To allow for these laser-guided SACLOS (semi-automatic command to line of sight) missiles to be guided using the tank's FCS, the LRF was replaced by the one also seen on the more modern Songun-915 (which is thought to contain the associated laser), and the gunner's optics were likely adapted. The SAM launcher, which can fire two MANPADS of any type in North Korean service, does not appear to be similarly integrated into the tank's FCS, as it features an entirely different engagement envelope. Instead, it uses a separate camera mounted on top of the launcher which allows a crew member to fire the system from inside. The massive proliferation of MANPADS in North Korea and their eventual fitting to even its most modern MBTs reflects the difficulty the DPRK is likely to have in defending their forces from enemy aircraft during a potential war, and this uniquely North Korean way of attempting to remedy the issue could become a serious headache especially for low-flying aircraft and helicopters. Last but not least, the tried-and-trusted KPV mounted to practically every tank in KPA service was replaced by a dual AGL based on its 1997 copy of the AGS-17, and a new sight was installed on top of the loader's hatch to operate this bulky system from within the tank. Though the AGS-17 is clearly at the basis of the design, there is some indication the calibre was actually beefed up, possibly to 40mm. Given that the AGL is vehicle-mounted, the negative consequences this has for weight and recoil would be largely negated. The decision to install this heavy system was likely made in order to increase its anti-infantry capabilities, against which AGLs can be especially lethal, while the KPV's AA capability was compensated for by the dual MANPADS system.

The weapons package does much to broaden the Chonma-216's scope of operations, and notably minimises crew exposure, a trend that is seen amongst modern MBT designs of many nations. Nonetheless, it also greatly increases the tank's visibility, and is likely to tack-on significant weight. Additionally, the types of weaponry installed are actually also indicative of the gaps in North Korean military technology. For instance, the ability to fire ATGMs through the main gun has been present on modern tanks of other militaries for decades, and the presence of better air defences or aerial superiority would negate the need for individual AA capabilities. Therefore, it could be argued that two other modifications on this new Chonma-216 variant are actually more representative of North Korean advancements in MBT technology. For one, the hull front has now been fitted with ERA tiles, indicating increased availability of this effective means of tank protection, and possibly preluding a wider deployment of the system. The other modification consists of two laser warning receiver (LWR) systems fitted to the smoke grenade dischargers on either side. These detect the laser emissions that are used to guide many anti-tank systems and automatically activate the smoke grenade dischargers to quickly lay down a defensive smoke screen. Known as a soft-kill active protection system (APS), these devices can greatly enhance a tank's survival chances against anti-tank systems, and might even feature an active component in the form of a laser dazzler which disables the emission source of laser-guided weaponry with bright laser flashes of its own.

After nearly three decades of trying to fully exploit the T-62's design to full advantage, the KPA finally switched to an altogether new tank line. The parade for the 65th anniversary of the Workers' Party of Korea in 2010 unveiled the first tank in serial production in the DPRK outfitted with a 125mm cannon for its main armament. The Songun-915 (US DoD designation 'M-2010'), first produced in 2009 (Juche 98), uses a chassis with several common characteristics of the Chonma-216, yet features many radical changes in the hull and turret. Aside from a more streamlined outlook, the hull has a redesigned engine deck and the driver's position is now centred – with both of the latter features clearly taking their design from the T-72. The turret superficially appears to copy the layout from the T-72, although it seems to be more spacious and use North Korean variants of the T-62's day and night optics for the gunner. The presence of a fourth crew member attests to the fact that the T-72's characteristic autoloader and ammunition carousel are absent, and the internal layout of the turret is likely more akin to the T-62 than the T-72. Curiously, the turret is welded together of sections of armour that seem themselves to have been cast, in theory combining the worst features of both welded and cast turrets into one, presumably for the sole reason that casting the turret in one piece was considered problematic. There is no telling if it has benefitted from developments in composite armour, though its appreciable thickness is apparent in various places. The turret also

A Chonma-216 with new weapons package during the 70th anniversary of the foundation of the DPRK parade in September 2018. The SAM station can retract to a forward position, but the tank's conspicuousness is nevertheless greatly increased. (NK Pro)

A detailed shot of the Chonma-216's new weapons package. Note what appears to be a LWR system directly behind the smoke grenade dischargers, and the redesigned LRF which can guide ATGMs. (NK Pro)

features a large extension towards the rear, not unlike that on the rarely seen Chonma designs of the 1980s, which is likely used for the storage of ammunition and/or tools, spares and accessories (the kits ordinarily found on top of the tracks were replaced by additional fuel tanks). It is outfitted with four smoke grenade dischargers on either side of the turret, a wind sensor, loudspeakers and the legacy IR searchlight which is retained from the Chonma. Like nearly all of North Korea's tank designs, it sports the heavy 14.5mm KPV on the turret. The LRF has been replaced by a new, smaller model, presumably due to the upgrade to a 125mm cannon. This cannon bears much resemblance to the T-72's D-81T(M) and is indeed derived from it, but mysteriously retains some very subtle characteristics of the U-5TS. Its exact capabilities also depend on the quality of the munitions North Korea is able to produce, but the mere increase in calibre is surely beneficial both to its armour piercing and high explosive (HE) shells. It is unclear whether separate charges and rounds are utilised (as on the T-72); the alternative of a massive unified munition is still likely to significantly impede loading speed. The Songun-915 also brings back ERA on the DPRK's tanks, installed on the hull and often (but not always) the turret. This thick turret ERA is quoted by North Korean sources as providing '500mms of protection' on top of the turret's protection value of '900mm', resulting in a total of '1400mm protection'.[20] [21] The ERA on the Songun-915 only covers its hull and turret front, and a small portion of the turret's top side, enhancing its protection from the front and against top-down munitions without adding too much weight or increasing overall cost. The North Korean source goes on to describe various other aspects of the Songun-915 in full detail, ascribing it with an integrated nuclear, biological and chemical (NBC) suite and the ability of fording through rivers at up to 1.8 metres depth, which is enlarged to five metres depth when using fording equipment.[22] Its 1,200 horsepower engine supposedly allows it to reach speeds of up to 70 kilometres per hour.[23] Even though it is somewhat unlikely that this is indeed the case considering the fact that the T-72's V-46 engine developing 780 horsepower was the best they had access to, many other values taken from these sources appear to be well within reasonable ranges. Notably, the weight of the tank is stated to be 44 tonnes, which is definitely plausible given the T-72 'Ural''s 41 tonnes.

Similar to the weapons package installed on the Chonma-216, evidence of weapons upgrades for the Songun-915 were first evident during the opening of the KPA Exhibition of Arms and Equipment in 2012. Nonetheless, only during the February 2018 parade for the 70th anniversary of the foundation of the Korean People's Army was this variant spotted in a seemingly operational capacity. Using the same dual AGL and MANPADS mounts as on the Chonma-216, although the latter is placed on the turret rear in the case of the Songun-915, the main difference is in the ATGM launcher in front of the commander's cupola. Much sturdier and cleaner in its design, this automated launcher appears to carry two Bulsae-5 ATGMs, which are thought to be guided through the gunner's optics. Curiously, the laser for the system already seems to have been integrated with the LRF, perhaps suggesting that the addition of ATGMs to this tank was always intended. The addition of the launcher indicates that even on the Songun-915 the ability to fire GLATGMs has not yet been mastered however, which was perhaps a too costly and specialised technology for the North Koreans. Nevertheless, the addition of two heavy ATGMs would be of much use during chance encounters with heavy armour of the South, against which the Songun-915 would otherwise be unlikely to achieve any penetration from the front. As on the Chonma-216, the new weapons package forfeits the 14.5mm KPV, and although it is reported to include the same passive protection system, with LWR, this has not yet been spotted.[24] As a whole, it provides the Songun-915 with a degree of versatility not seen on any other MBT anywhere on the globe, at the cost of additional weight and much increased visibility.

Production of these later generations of MBTs has continued concurrently yet intermittently. The new six-wheeled chassis, and larger derivatives, is nowadays also used as the basis for other hardware – most notably ballistic missiles and artillery – their production has stymied and at times entirely halted the output of Chonma-216s and Songun-915s of the Kusong tank factory. In the first years after its inception, it appears difficulties with the Songun-915's 125mm cannon also complicated its introduction, and since Chonma-216 production was preceded by small-scale manufacture of the Chonma-214 and Chonma-215, some few dozens of each type, the size of their production runs remain difficult to estimate accurately. Nonetheless, careful scrutiny of serial numbers visible during parades and exercises suggests that the combined numbers for the Chonma-214, 215, 216 and Songun-915 are at least some 190. Why both the Chonma-216 and the Songun-915 continued to be produced alongside is unclear in the first place, as it could be

A Songun 915 MBT fitted with ERA to its hull front and its turret. (NK Pro)

One of the first improvements over the original Chonma design came in the form of an extended rear section. While only a modest improvement to an at that time already outdated design, it showed that North Korea's ambitions were already outgrowing the design limitations of the original turret. The tank seen here is equipped with attachment points for slat armour around the turret, hull and sides. (Artwork by David Bocquelet)

By the time the production of the original Chonma model was well underway South Korea was already in the process of fielding the far superior K1 MBT. Having lost the advantage in MBTs it previously held, North Korean tank designers now found themselves playing catch-up to match its modern design. The development of several Chonma models sporting a new angular turret would form the basis of this North Korean effort and subsequent tank design until the introduction of the Songun-915 in 2009. Seen here is the mysterious Chonma with a thermal sleeve and possibly a 125mm cannon. (Artwork by David

The Chonma-214 was the last North Korean tank design to make use of the T-62's original five road wheel chassis. As an intermediate model following the Chonma-92 and Chonma-98, the Chonma-214 is believed to have enjoyed a relatively limited production run before the advent of the Chonmas featuring six road wheels. Nonetheless, many of the features on the Chonma-214 would later be incorporated into the designs of the Chonma-215, Chonma-216 and the Songun-915. Also note the appliqué armour on the front of the turret and the altered front drive wheel. (Artwork by David Bocquelet)

While the Chonma-215 is nearly identical in general design to the Chonma-216, the two tanks can easily be discerned by the T-62-style chassis with one additional axle on the Chonma-215 and the T-72-inspired chassis on the Chonma-216. Produced just a year before the introduction of the superior Chonma-216, the real purpose of this tank might have been nothing more than a feasibility study into adapting the Chonma chassis to one that features six road wheels, introducing several key advancements in North Korean tank design in the process. (Artwork by David Bocquelet)

Named in honour of Kim Jong Il's birthday, the Chonma-216 is the last North Korean tank design to make use of the 115mm cannon of the T-62. Strikingly different from the original Chonma variant first produced in 1976, its Chonma designation is perhaps unappreciative for all the changes it incorporates. Nonetheless, it is likely that even its many improvements could not redeem the lack of a new 125mm main gun, effectively killing any prospects of mass production before the design was even finished. However, as difficulties with the new 125mm gun are believed to have plagued the Songun-915's development, the production run of the Chonma-216 might have run longer than originally envisaged. (Artwork by David Bocquelet)

Like the Chonma-216 before it, the Songun-915 is an odd blend of T-62 and T-72 technologies merged together. Though it was produced in not insignificant numbers, it is uncertain if the design was ever truly successful. (Artwork by David Bocquelet)

The main hall of the KPA Exhibition of Arms and Equipment in Pyongyang. Weaponry tracing back to the early days of the KPA as well as many of the DPRK's indigenous projects are showcased here to a select audience. (NK Pro)

A Songun-915 with new weapons package during the 70th anniversary of the foundation of the DPRK parade in September 2018. Note the large Bulsae-5 ATGMs, which differ from the ATGMs mounted on the Chonma-216. (NK Pro)

expected to have complicated the production process for either model. Nevertheless, the introduction of these new tank designs was definitely more than just a token effort, and it is estimated that by the mid 2010s some dozens of the Chonma-216 and Songun-915 were being produced per year each, albeit with frequent interruptions.

Rather than developing further variants of its still brand-new Songun-915, North Korea in a surprise move unveiled another all-new MBT design (tentatively dubbed M-2020 by some) during the 75th anniversary of the Workers' Party of Korea parade in 2020. Despite having almost no technological debt to the Chonma series of tanks, its designation was later revealed to be the Chonma-2. In yet another recent instance of intentional mimicry of foreign designs, the tank instead bears a clear resemblance to the Russian T-14 Armata and US M1 Abrams, borrowing hull features and design philosophies from the former and the angular extended turret from the latter. Despite the similarities, the Chonma-2 underneath is still very much North Korean, and implements various design solutions that hearken back to the Soviet tank technologies that were available to its engineers, while attempting to move towards a more Western philosophy of design.

The hull retains many T-72 influences also present on the Songun-915, with much of the engine deck and rear copied over directly and the driver's position in the centre of the vehicle. Towards the front, the hull starts to differ more significantly, with seven road wheels of slightly smaller size than the Songun-915's slightly lengthening and lowering the chassis. The tracks themselves suggest further innovation, with the single-pin track links making way for a double-pin design that should be capable of more easily bearing the weight of the new MBT's heavy armour. As on the Armata, an arrangement of bolts on the glacis plate gives the impression that ERA was seamlessly incorporated into the exterior, yet unlike the Armata there is no readily apparent way of removing or replacing this ERA when expended – if it indeed constitutes ERA.

Though the thick frontal aspect plating and armoured side skirts must contribute significantly to the Chonma-2's weight, the turret is likely to cause the bulk of the weight increase over the Songun-915. The main armament appears to consist of a modified D-81T 125mm cannon, but like on some Western MBT designs, a muzzle reference system has been fitted to measure tiny deformations of the barrel due to temperature and wear and automatically pass this information on to the FCS. Additionally, the barrel appears to be slightly longer than on the Songun-915. Given the apparent troubles with the 125mm cannon on the Songun-915 and other Western influences in modern North Korean weaponry, it is possible that a 120mm cannon was opted for instead, although there would be no obvious foreign source for this technology. Whatever the case, it uses unitary munitions so the loader does not have to load the charge and shell separately, and a HEAT and armour-piercing fin-stabilised discarding-sabot round are known to have been developed. Situated above this cannon, the LRF found on all North Korean indigenous tanks of the past decades was miniaturised further to a relatively compact device.

The internal layout of the tank appears substantially altered compared to previous generations, matching modern manually-loaded MBTs of other nations. Effectively, this mirrors the crew's positions; the coaxial machine gun usually present on the right hand side of the turret was removed, and a cutout in the armour on the left hand side where the gunner's optics are usually located is likely reserved for it instead. The gunner's optics are now housed in a separate bulky device on the right hand side, of the same type also found on North Korea's new wheeled gun system. Though it is similar in layout to the SOSNA-U utilised on modern Russian tanks, it has unique features that suggest an indigenous development. While its performance is hence unknown, merely the fact that it represents the first substantial improvement in tank sights and ostensibly a switch from active to passive (and/or thermal) night vision means a veritable leap in performance.

The turret rear features a range of other sensors thought to be associated with the FCS, including the wind sensor also seen on the Chonma-215 onwards. The fact that the tried-and-trusted KPV was exchanged for an AGL (operable from within the tank) affixed to the loader's hatch means the tank's AA capability, so prized on other North Korean armoured fighting vehicles (AFVs), was entirely forfeited. An additional digitised optic bolted atop the armour just left of the main gun is believed to provide a modest measure of forward-facing visibility for when the AGL is used while buttoned-up. The dual SAM launcher of the modernised Chonma-216 and Songun-915 is not present on this tank, saving some space on the already crowded turret. Secondary armament consists of a dual ATGM launcher with two Bulsae-5s attached to the side of the turret, which uses hydraulics to switch between travel and fire mode. The system's optics appear to be fused with the commander's optics, which is a separate, even bulkier, combined optic mounted to the commander's hatch that can be rotated along with it for a 360° view. The rear section of the turret is likely reserved for tools, spares and accessories: compartmentalised storage of ammunition is unlikely, and the panels atop seem to be ill configured to function as blowout panels.[25] Another highly conspicuous feature of the turret is a hard-kill APS consisting of four separate radars and four sets of three launch tubes protruding from the turret sides. These tubes contain the charges that are meant to disrupt incoming penetrators when detected by the radar system, in so doing increasing the odds of survival. The APS is matched by the same soft-kill system with LWRs and smoke grenade dischargers seen on other new North Korean AFVs, fitted behind slat armour that doubles as a bustle rack and completes the similarity with the Abrams tank. To provide additional protection from the top-attack munitions that are nowadays widely available on the battlefield, thick armour, possibly containing built-in ERA, lines the turret roof. Much like on the Armata, angular plating hides the true shape of the armour on the turret front and sides, housing the APS and simultaneously providing a degree of spaced armour protection. During the parade commemorating the 70th anniversary of the Fatherland Liberation War in July 2023 it became apparent that North Korea is still exploring methods to further enhance the Chonma-2's armour protection, as demonstrated by the installation of additional ERA around the turret and on the sides.

Accompanying the introduction of the new MBT and subsequent modifications is new equipment and clothing for tank crews, some components of which seem to be making their way to crews of older tank models as well, emphasising that the North's mechanised modernisation efforts are substantive rather than merely symbolic. Perhaps the most important component of this new gear are the tank helmets with integrated headsets, which are thought to be part of a tank battlefield management system that allows both improved communications amongst the crews and with other vehicles on the battlefield. Nevertheless, these introductions have remained sporadic, with some of the Chonma-2's crews spotted during exercises with traditional outfits.

While the Chonma-2 represents perhaps the single most important leap in MBT technology in decades, much about its precise characteristics remains unknown or even highly questionable. Tellingly, for the 2020, 2021 and 2022 parades examples with the same serial numbers were paraded, suggesting production had not advanced beyond this initial batch – with Korean Central

The Chonma-2 during the February 2023 parade. Parades in the early 2020s saw these tanks sporting yellowish, then olive green and lastly beige camouflages. (KCBC)

Bulsae-5 ATGMs are fired from the dual launcher mounted on the side of the Chonma-2's turret. At least two out of eight participating Chonma-2s suffered significant damage to their side skirts in this exercise. (KCBC)

The active protection system of the Chonma-2 undergoes testing against an incoming rocket-propelled grenade. The prohibitive cost of such systems is likely to significantly restrict their widespread adoption. (KCBC)

The crew of the Chonma-2 in this parade is equipped with new tanker gear that offers significantly improved ergonomics compared to the older gear, which has remained practically unchanged since the 1950s. (KCBC)

Kim Jong Un inspects the day and night optics and crew multi-function displays of the Chonma-2 during a visit to the Academy of Defence Sciences in May 2024. (KCBC)

The Chonma-2 MBT represents a leap in technological maturity, and is the first North Korean MBT no longer to include clear elements from the T-62. Despite its radically modern look and some advanced features however, it still has various parts of its design in common with the T-72. The new MBT is presented in its upgraded configuration, featuring explosive reactive armour encasing the turret and sides. The tank is also among the few KPAGF MBTs to feature military camouflage, with several different patterns having been displayed. (Artwork by Anderson Subtil)

North Korea's latest (as yet unnamed) MBT unshackles itself from virtually any link to a Soviet or Russian predecessor. Although lending much of its layout from the Chonma-2 unveiled just four years earlier, critical components like the engine, armour, APS and much of the turret have been completely redesigned. While its various components had not yet been demonstrated in early 2025, if fully functional the design might be capable of going toe-to-toe with some of the South's most modern MBT designs. (Artwork by Anderson Subtil)

News Agency (KCNA) commentary on the 2020 parade explicitly declaring them to be prototypes. The North Korean approach to AFV development can be described as iterative in the sense that seemingly operational weapons still get worked on, and differences between production vehicles might be introduced as the precise design is finalised. Only since 2023 did examples with new serial numbers start to be displayed, and an increase in demonstrations of the tank's various systems suggested that they were ready to enter active service. Tellingly, the aesthetics of components like the APS were subtly different in these iterations. Moreover, an apparent command tank variant features various modifications including antennas for additional radio equipment. Meanwhile, North Korean state media suggested the MBTs had entered service with the 105th Tank Division, with evidence suggesting the existence of at least 26 Chonma-2s as of mid 2024.[26] Serious teething problems clearly remain, and a May 2025 inspection of the Kusong tank plant revealed that the barrels of eight field-tested Chonma-2s had been removed again.

Furthermore, indications remained that the DPRK was not yet entirely satisfied with the performance of its newest, Western-influenced design. During a 2024 visit by Kim Jong Un to the Academy of Defence Sciences, alongside a model of the Chonma-2 a prototype engine was displayed that is closely patterned after the German MT 883 diesel engine. Exactly how this design could have been copied is uncertain; with only few AFVs utilising it some type of security breach cannot be excluded. Its display next to the Chonma-2 model was similarly curious, with that type evidently

Kim Jong Un inspects an engine closely patterned after the German MTU MT 883, which is itself very similar to the Doosan DV27K that powers the South Korean K2 Black Panther MBT. In the background, models of a 323-based 120mm SPM and a new wheeled gun system. (KCBC)

still utilising an engine derived from that of the T-72. The integration of the MT 883 copy would certainly be a massive improvement, with some power packs that utilise it developing upwards of 1,500hp, but such a retrofit might prove problematic. Moreover, establishing mass production of engines in this class and their associated transmissions is anything but simple, with both South Korea and Türkiye having significant difficulties in manufacturing indigenous alternatives for the MT 883 in their own MBTs. However, the introduction of this engine or derivatives on future AFVs fielded by the KPA could have far-ranging consequences for their performance and design specifications.

A Glocom schematic of a generic (M1A2 Abrams) tank showcasing the command version of its tank battlefield management system. (Glocom)

A novel engine should of course have drawn attention to the possibility of a new MBT being in the works. Less than five years after the unveiling of one of the modest radical departures from North Korean MBT design heritage, there are few who might have seriously entertained the idea however. Yet it is precisely what would occur next, with the 'National Defence Development-2024' exhibition serving as the backdrop for the unveiling of the as yet unnamed tank. In many ways, the vehicle continues along the path delineated by the Chonma-2's innovations, now seemingly expunging virtually any trace of a Soviet heritage in its design. This departure is coupled by what are almost certainly a set of modifications aimed at incorporating lessons gleaned from the performance of various MBT designs in the Russo-Ukrainian War and other post-2020 conflicts. Meanwhile, many of the elements debuted on the Chonma-2 were retained or improved, resulting in what in theory should be a highly capable MBT. The chassis' changes revolve largely around the rear deck, reflecting the swap to the DPRK's copy of the MT 883 as its engine. The full power pack moreover seems to include a transmission closely patterned after the South Korean EST15K, again raising questions about its origin. Due to its impressive compactness, the length of the vehicle remains largely unchanged. The additional power seems to have permitted a slightly reinforced glacis however, and the side skirt armour package introduced on the uprated Chonma-2 was exchanged for a bulky ERA layout. Changes to the turret are especially extensive. The Chonma-2's turret-embedded APS has been replaced by a completely new system, resembling the Israeli Iron Fist or the Chinese GL-6 in its operating mode. Two conspicuous launchers each loaded with four interceptors are bolted to the turret bustle (which is slightly narrower yet higher), providing all-aspect coverage. Acquisition is still achieved through a set of four radars, now completely embedded in a bulky kit of add-on armour (with hinges to allow for armour inserts) that significantly increases the turret's protection. While radar coverage is improved compared to the Chonma-2, a gap remains facing backwards. Nevertheless, the advantages offered by this set-up are obvious: while possibly conceding performance against direct-fire weapons, the MBT is now also protected from top-attack munitions. Given that such munitions nowadays constitute perhaps the single greatest threat to well-armoured AFVs, the payoff should be well worth it. Further attention to top-attack munitions is given in the distribution of the turret ERA, which solely covers weak spots on the turret top and no longer the turret sides. The crew configuration appears to be unaltered from the Chonma-2, but still greater emphasis is placed on capabilities while buttoned-up. To this end, the commander's sight now consists of a stand-alone panoramic sight, with the commander's cupola featuring periscope sights in every direction but backwards as a backup. Furthermore, cameras appear to be fitted in the turret's side armour for enhanced situational awareness. Similarly, the loader's 40mm AGL is now a true remote weapon station (RWS), fitted on its own rotating mount and integrated with a set of day and night optics. The same RWS was also shown on the model of one of North Korea's new mobile gun systems, hinting at a broader introduction of this compact design. Meanwhile, the gunner's sights have remained largely the same albeit slightly more compact, and the coaxial machine gun was moved back to the right hand side of the turret for uncertain reasons. The main gun itself appears to be of the same make as the Chonma-2's, including the same LRF and muzzle reference device. Other features like the dual ATGM launcher (albeit with a simplified construction), LWRs and various sensors were also retained, while the number of smoke grenade dischargers was increased to six on either side. In the hull, the driver's visibility while driving with the hatches closed was improved by the introduction of an additional periscope and what is believed to be a rotating night vision device.

The resulting vehicle may certainly be considered the most ambitious undertaking in tank design in North Korea ever, and a solid attempt at producing an MBT that is in step with other designs currently entering the market. In particular, it is a serious contender for the K2 family, with features like an emphasis on situational awareness and active protection systems seemingly intended to match that type. Of course, the new tank's true effectiveness will be determined by the quality of its components, with especially aspects like sensor fusion, sensitivity and versatility of optics, reliability and efficacy of the APS (and various weapons systems) being very hard to ascertain. Moreover, with the DPRK now moving towards more conventional approaches to modern tank design in terms of situational awareness, C4ISR (command, control, communications, computers, intelligence, surveillance and reconnaissance) integration and the extensive set of electronics that such systems entail, it will have to make radical investments in its high tech industry to attain substantial production volumes. While its modern arms industry is continuously proving that it has not failed to observe the importance of these technologies, it will likely remain difficult to do so without relying on allies with more mature electronics industries like China. These difficulties were underlined in state media coverage of a May 2025 inspection of the Kusong tank plant, with photos of the event doctored to show four more MBTs than were actually present. Moreover, the one intact vehicle on display was the same prototype unveiled at the 'National Defence Development-2024' exhibition; a second article remained unfinished beyond the chassis.

Aside from the introduction of new tanks, some effort has gone into upgrading older examples as well. Although much of its T-55 and T-62-based inventories remain unmodified, some examples have been spotted with added smoke grenade dischargers in order to enhance their survivability at low cost. Furthermore, there is some indication a programme for overhauling T-55 pattern tanks with armour upgrades, new side skirts and a weapons package similar to that seen on the newest Chonma-216s and Songun-915s, aside from upgrades to its FCS and sensor suite that can only be guessed at, was under development. This would do much to increase the effectiveness of these by now thoroughly obsolete MBTs, but it remains to be seen whether sufficient resources and production capacity can be mustered to actually execute such plans. In the meantime, the possibility that this upgrade programme is solely offered as an export venture appears to be the most likely.

A view showcasing the new MBT's turret rear. The new APS's launchers can be easily discerned as the tank's tallest feature, straddling the remodelled turret bustle with various sensors and smoke grenade dischargers. (KCBC)

A side view of the DPRK's newest MBT at the 'National Defence Development-2024' exhibition. Note the hefty ERA package on the side skirts and very substantial turret side armour with embedded radars and sensors. (KCBC)]

An opposing view of the same prototype at the Kusong tank plant, showcasing the optics and armaments on the turret front. The tank in the background appears to have photoshopped in. (KCBC)]

Shown side by side are a Chonma-216 and the Chonma-2. With at most 16 years separating their introductions, it is evident that North Korean tank design has advanced rapidly. (KCBC)]

2

ARTILLERY

The KPA is quick to flaunt its prestigious tank forces, air force and navy in various propaganda settings and exercises. Still, there are few occasions on which as many personnel, and as much materiel and raw firepower are brought to bear as during a combined artillery exercise of the KPA. The ground trembles as hundreds of artillery pieces and multiple rocket launchers (MRLs) simultaneously unleash their fury on distant targets in a carefully choreographed display of military might – as much an opportunity to practise mobilisation and tactics such Time On Target fire as it is a propaganda statement.[1] Although the concentration of fire during such exercises is often exaggerated for effect, to the extent of individual shells/rockets hitting and detonating one another in the air over the target, they are in fact but a taste of what can be expected during wartime operations. With some 8,800 artillery pieces larger than 76mm and 5,500 MRLs in active service, North Korea boasts the largest artillery forces in the world, surpassing even powers such as China, Russia and the USA. These unparalleled masses of equipment have been built up through well over half a century of arms acquisition and production, and its current composition still reflects every stage of that process. Second World War vintage artillery pieces serve alongside modern long-ranged precision-guided MRLs, presenting serious logistical challenges as well as creating a strange contrast between the equipment of some units versus others.[2]

Nonetheless, its strength lies in numbers and the threat of the KPA's artillery forces is often regarded as a deterrent in its own right alongside the North's weapons of mass destruction – supposedly capable of razing Seoul to the ground in short notice. Aside from the questionable military benefit of such a strategy, this long-standing rumour is verifiably false; it nevertheless serves well to illustrate their notoriety abroad. Especially its vast arsenal of MRLs is unmatched by any other nation, and they are capable of bearing an incredible amount of firepower on a target within short notice, at the cost of being a heavy drain on logistics. In the initial stages of a war the artillery stationed along the DMZ would commence a massive barrage aimed at suppressing and disabling enemy defences, themselves drawing upon hundreds of Hardened Artillery Sites (HARTS) built just above the DMZ to increase their survivability against counter-battery fire. What artillery pieces that are capable of moving on their own volition then follow the main offensive into the South, with towed artillery lagging behind with slower infantry units. Despite the large numbers of self-propelled guns (SPGs) and self-propelled MRLs, equally large numbers of towed artillery pieces and MRLs also see service with the KPA, and prior to the 1970s virtually comprised the whole of its artillery forces. The KPA, from the onset supplied by the Soviet Union which despite practically introducing the MRL did not produce many dedicated self-propelled artillery pieces until after the Second World War, was traditionally an infantry-centred force supported by towed artillery and tanks. Although lacking in SPGs, the KPA did operate some types of imported Soviet and Chinese MRLs. Some of these, such as the famous 132mm BM-13, the 200mm BMD-20 and 240mm BM-24, were of Second World War vintage, delivered during and just after the Korean War by the Soviet Union. Others, most notably the ubiquitous 122mm BM-21 and Chinese 107mm Type-63 towed MRL, were delivered during the late 1960s, greatly increasing the gap in capabilities between the North and South of the peninsula. Even though these systems represent some of the oldest equipment of its type, they are still in use with the KPA to this day, often featuring in parades and exercises.

During the modernisation and mechanisation of the KPA in the 1970s it was believed that the North's army would advance

240mm BM-24 MRLs parading directly behind APCs equipped with 122mm launch tubes. The two types of artillery were produced more than half a century apart. (KCBC)]

so fast into the South that towed artillery was liable to get left behind, and a push for mobilising its artillery force was initiated that would eventually lead to the vastly diverse arsenal of SPGs and MRLs seen today. Still, even before this point the DPRK had a significant artillery advantage over the South, both in numbers and capabilities. In part, this can be attributed to a very early endeavour to produce its own artillery, even to the point of designing a unique 76mm cannon that was used in the coastal defence role. Although this calibre even in those early days was underwhelming for such a weapon, the undertaking was anything if not impressive for a fledgling indigenous industry, and North Korea seems to value the design to the point of still using an anti-tank variant mounted on the 323 APC. Starting in the 1960s, its highly successful indigenous production of such field guns and howitzers as the Soviet 122mm D-30 and 130mm M-46 (known as the Type-68) greatly boosted its ranks, with the latter – whose 27 kilometre range was for years unparalleled – especially threatening to the ROKA and United States Forces Korea, and laid the foundation for a variety of indigenous designs that would see the light of day in later years. The most widespread of these also leaned on other Soviet designs such as the 122mm D-74, 152mm D-20 and the powerful 130mm SM-4-1 coastal artillery gun, which had a range of close to 30 kilometres and is therefore still highly favoured in KPA service. Two more indigenous designs, a copy of the 122mm D-74 and the other sharing a close resemblance to the Romanian 152mm A411, shedding light on the two nations' military cooperation, would be prolifically produced and exported. The North's towed artillery made its way to many of its former export partners, including such nations as Egypt, Libya, Lebanon, Uganda, Vietnam, DR Congo and Madagascar. Many of its artillery guns and howitzers were ideally suited for mounting on a mobile chassis and would require little to no modification in the years hence for the self-propelled gun/howitzer role. Its towed artillery industry also had offshoots in the form of several anti-tank gun designs, which are still widely employed today. Despite its prolific indigenous production, like in any branch of the KPA several Korean War and even Second World War relics still continue service, mostly with reserves. These include anything from the 57mm ZiS-2 anti-tank gun to heavy 152mm ML-20 howitzers.

North Korea's first attempts at mobilising artillery pieces can be traced back to the late 1960s, when at least two types of artillery pieces were mounted on the Soviet ATS-59 artillery tractor chassis. These contraptions also emphasised the sincere intent of setting up an indigenous industry for the production of military equipment, considering the fact that while one of the artillery pieces used was the Soviet-legacy 152mm D-20 howitzer-gun, the other was a homebred improvement of the 130mm M-46 field gun sporting the muzzle brake of the SM-4-1 coastal defence gun of the same calibre. This modified design would remain popular in subsequent years and ultimately be used on nearly every generation of SPGs produced by the DPRK.

During the 1970s the programme of indigenously designing self-propelled artillery advanced dramatically with the introduction of three common types of chassis. The first of these, designated Tokchon in North Korea, was still based on the ATS-59 artillery tractor, although its superstructure had been heavily modified into a form more dedicated to the artillery role and equipped with thin sheet armour against shrapnel damage. Throughout the 1970s at least three different artillery systems were mounted onto this chassis, constituting five SPG designs. The first of these, according to North Korean sources conceived in 1972 and described in Western sources as the M-1974 or M-1977, used an indigenously designed 152mm howitzer-gun based on the Soviet D-20, but with a modified muzzle brake.[3] This gun, and this SPG, are especially prolific in KPA service, providing heavy firepower over relatively short range. Two other Tokchon-based SPGs, one with a partially enclosed turret conceived in 1974 and known in the West as the M-1991 or M-1992, and another without (M-1975 or M-1981), used the aforementioned 130mm indigenous M-46 inspired field gun. Another Tokchon-type SPG carried an indigenous 122mm field gun, and was supposedly conceived in 1978 (US DoD designation M-1981).[4] Presumably the last and most modern SPG of this class originated somewhere in the early 1980s and once again used the indigenous 152mm howitzer-gun, yet this time in a completely enclosed turret in line with developments on other chassis at the time. This type is often described in Western sources as the M-1985 or M-1991 and is still one of the most modern SPGs used by the KPA, albeit one that is spotted rarely.

A North Korean 130mm SM-4-1 used in the coastal defence role. (KCBC)

An indigenous 152mm gun-howitzer is inspected by Kim Jong Un during KPA artillery exercises. This howitzer closely resembles the Romanian 152mm A411. (KCBC)

Above: 152mm Tokchon-based SPGs during a KPA artillery exercise. Note the crew sitting behind the vehicle, operating the 152mm gun-howitzer as they would a towed artillery piece. (KCBC)

Left: A turreted 152mm Tokchon-based SPG during exercises in 2016. This variant is still operated with the crew sitting outside. (KCBC)

Tokchon-based SPGs armed with 130mm guns derived from the SM-4-1 during the 60th anniversary of the Korean War armistice parade in 2013. These are of a different, more common variant than the one in the previous image, underlining the massive variety of SPGs in KPA service. (KCBC)

A Tokchon-based SPG armed with a 122mm gun based on the D-74 during the 100th anniversary of Kim Il Sung's birthday parade in 2012. (David Flack)

Another well-known and broadly exported early SPG design was based on the 323 APC platform and is one of the few that uses the light 122mm D-30 howitzer in a virtually unmodified form. It has been in production since 1976 (US DoD designation M-1977), with a second slightly improved variant featuring a modified muzzle brake and subtly redesigned hull seeing light sometime in the 1980s (US DoD designation M-1985). The M-1985 appears to have either largely supplanted its predecessor or been produced in greater numbers as it is the only one of the two to be featured in any recent parades or exercises. Nonetheless, the earlier M-1977 variant was one of the first of many North Korean artillery designs to be exported. Delivered to Ethiopia in 1985, it subsequently saw heavy use by Ethiopian forces during the Eritrean War of Independence and the following Eritrean-Ethiopian War.

A Tokchon-based SPG armed with a 130mm gun based on the SM-4-1. Notice the large spades used to brace the vehicle against recoil. (KCBC)

An M-1985 122mm SPG during the 60th anniversary of the Korean People's Army parade in 1992. Note the quadruple MANPADS launcher, whose operability is questionable. (KCBC)

M-1977 122mm SPGs used by Ethiopia. (KCBC)

The availability of several mobile chassis and indigenously designed anti-tank guns was also swiftly applied to the production of a range of different tank destroyers of varying sophistication. At least three of these have entered service in significant numbers, of which a 76mm gun mounted to the back of a 323 APC should be counted as the least impressive, providing little more than light fire support. As early as 1972, a 100mm anti-tank gun was also mounted on the Tokchon and 323 chassis, although only the former appears to have entered actual production. This vehicle likely serves in large numbers, and has even been spotted equipped with a LRF for enhanced efficacy over long ranges. Still, it is thinly armoured and its 100mm gun, though powerful, is no match for the armour of actual MBTs. A third, much more rare design supposedly uses a mysterious 103mm gun about which very little is known. Based on a heavily modified 323 APC, it features seldomly in exercises despite reportedly being produced since 1974.[5] A range of prototypes based on various types of chassis also exist that do not appear to have entered service. Of particular interest are a triad of casemated guns, which albeit an interesting avenue of approach in modern tank destroyer design, are unlikely to have been very successful. Similarly, a large casemate-type tank destroyer seen inspected by Kim Il Sung somewhere in the early 1970s does not appear to have made its way into the KPA's arsenal. Curiously, this type came equipped with firing ports for the crew manning the 100mm gun.

The mobilisation of artillery pieces was paired with that of a variety of mortars, evolving from the simple truck-based mortar teams used as early as the Korean War. Although most types simply mounted an 82mm or 120mm mortar in an open-topped 323 APC, with the start of production dating back to 1976 and 1978 respectively, one stands out as a self-propelled mortar (SPM) that bears much resemblance to the Soviet 120mm 2S9 Nona. Unlike this similarly turreted design, the North Korean SPM is based around an indigenous 140mm mortar and uses a modified 323 chassis for propulsion. First seen during the parade for the 60th anniversary of the Korean People's Army in 1992, this vehicle was first produced in 1981, although its relative rarity in propaganda material suggests

A Tokchon-based 100mm tank destroyer. Note the LRF also mounted on Syrian T-55s upgraded by North Korea, indicating an improved FCS on this example. (KCBC)

Kim Il Sung inspecting an indigenously produced B-10 recoilless rifle. In the back, one of the more elusive and curious AFV designs ever to come from North Korea soil: a large casemate-style tank destroyer equipped with a 100mm cannon. Note the BTR-60-style firing ports that can be used by the crew. (KCBC)

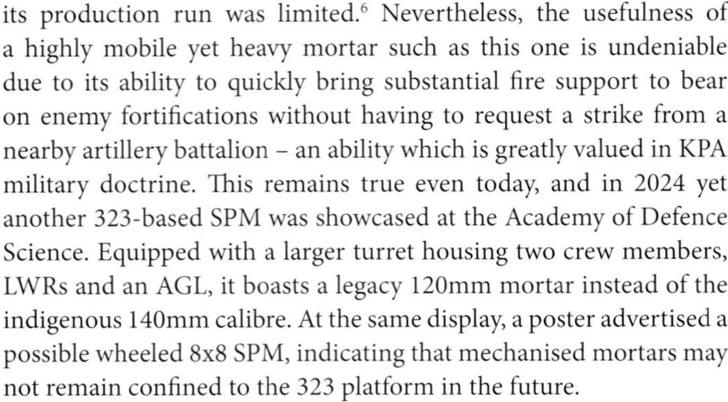

its production run was limited.[6] Nevertheless, the usefulness of a highly mobile yet heavy mortar such as this one is undeniable due to its ability to quickly bring substantial fire support to bear on enemy fortifications without having to request a strike from a nearby artillery battalion – an ability which is greatly valued in KPA military doctrine. This remains true even today, and in 2024 yet another 323-based SPM was showcased at the Academy of Defence Science. Equipped with a larger turret housing two crew members, LWRs and an AGL, it boasts a legacy 120mm mortar instead of the indigenous 140mm calibre. At the same display, a poster advertised a possible wheeled 8x8 SPM, indicating that mechanised mortars may not remain confined to the 323 platform in the future.

A 323-based 140mm SPM during the 60th anniversary of the Korean People's Army parade in 1992. (KCBC)

A scale model of a 323-based 120mm SPM. It is unknown if this type has actually been prototyped or (mass-)produced. (KCBC)

Due to the wide variety of SPG designs on a multitude of platforms produced by the DPRK, and of course the secrecy surrounding these projects, past intelligence on the matter has often been subject to confusion and misinformation. Things are complicated further by the existence of certain artillery systems that do not seem to fit into any known line of development, such as a rarely spotted SPG based on a platform that is best described as a hybrid of the Tokchon and 323 chassis, with a 122mm D-30 howitzer for its armament.[7] The fact that this system has never been seen outside a single propaganda video and is not known in any Western or even North Korean sources makes it extremely hard to guess whether or not the design was a success or if it has ever been produced in any significant numbers.

While some of the earlier Tokchon-type SPGs were exempt from this uncertain status due to large amounts of propaganda imagery, their featuring in parades and even North Korean sources describing their specifics, the second major iteration of SPGs launched during the 1980s was not. The Juche Po class of artillery is usually identified by a chassis counting six road wheels and a fully enclosed cupola, shielding most of the gun, and its operators, from small arms fire and shrapnel.[8] The most famous example in this series is known to the US DoD as the M-1991, and was featured in the parade for the 60th anniversary of the Korean People's Army in 1992, for a long time making it the only one of which clear imagery was available. It uses the same indigenous 122mm D-74-based field gun as the previously mentioned M-1981 Tokchon produced since 1978, albeit with a modified recoil and firing mechanism. The other main variant, known as the M-1992, was much more obscure, using a more modern remodelled turret housing what appears to be a new 130mm or 152mm gun. Notably, this SPG features a bore evacuator, greatly aiding in the reduction of fumes in the turret after firing. As a result, whereas the previous type has been spotted firing with its crew outside the vehicle, the M-1992 can likely execute artillery salvos while completely closed up, increasing its effectiveness. Although it was likely first produced in the early 1990s, it was displayed properly during the parade for the 70th anniversary of the foundation of the DPRK in September 2018 for the first time. Other variants of the Juche Po exist perhaps using different calibres and with slightly modified chassis and turret, but due to the extremely limited amount of imagery available not much else can be speculated about these systems, including whether they actually entered serial production. The M-1991 and M-1992 have been spotted during more recent exercises and parades however, and during the 2018 parades these were even seen upgraded with a new weapons package derived from the one seen on the Chonma-216 and Songun-915. Both the dual

The mysterious 'rubber duck' SPG, another testament to the diversity of the KPA's artillery platforms. (KCBC)

M-1991 122mm SPGs during the 105th anniversary of Kim Il Sung's birthday parade of 2017. (NK Pro)

M-1992 SPGs during the 70th anniversary of the foundation of the DPRK parade in September 2018. Note the extensive new weapons package mounted to the turret. (NK Pro)

MANPADS and dual AGL are fitted, complemented by 14 smoke grenade dischargers dispersed over the turret. These modifications reflect the fact that this SPG is to serve with frontline units such as Strike Forces, where situations where such armament will need to be used are not unthinkable. It is likely MANPADS launchers of a more rudimentary kind are to be mounted on other SPGs located in other rear areas vulnerable to aerial attack however, as is attested by examples carrying them during various parades of the past decades.

Indubitably the most famous and most ambitious of North Korea's SPGs is what is described by the US DoD as the 'M-1978 Koksan', confusingly designated by North Korean sources as the Chuch'e'po (literally 'Juche gun'), a name that would later also become the identifier of the aforementioned class of SPGs. This mysterious behemoth, armed with a monstrous indigenous 170mm gun with a barrel length of over eight metres, is based on a modified T-54/55 or Type-59 tank chassis and has supposedly been produced since 1973.[9] However, the truth behind its origin has so far remained elusive, and a range of prototypes produced in the 1970s and 1980s have not been documented. One of the factors that complicate research into the subject is the SPG's odd 170mm calibre; no known Soviet or Chinese – or Western for that matter – artillery uses this type of munition, severely limiting the Koksan's possible ancestry. The gun's unique design is also hard to trace back to any foreign artillery, suggesting the Koksan might have in fact been a fully indigenous project. This would have been highly impressive given its early date of introduction, and indeed the very slow initial production indicates that North Korea encountered great difficulty in producing it.[10] Theories about possible alternative origins for the Koksan vary wildly from some unknown type of Soviet coastal artillery to some even claiming it is based on a German Second World War-era 17cm field gun, presumably supplied to North Korea by the Soviet Union after the war had ended. Although a foreign design might have inspired the development of the Koksan, no one artillery piece can be linked to it, and the specifics around its creation are unlikely to ever come to light. The reasons for its creation are a lot less mysterious however. After the creation of the DMZ the need arose for an artillery piece that would be capable of shelling South Korean positions from well beyond the border, out of reach from retaliation by counter-artillery strikes.[11] The uncommon 170mm calibre likely has its origin in its attempt to squeeze as much range as possible out of the design. The gun, while in transport mode carried in the centre of its T-55-based chassis, can slide back and lean on the rear of the chassis, aided by two large collapsible spades to help cope with the massive recoil its munition demands. By using a thick barrel, an indigenously designed muzzle brake and a highly complex recoil and firing mechanism, the first mass-produced Koksan SPG can build up extremely high pressures and therefore attain an estimated range of some 43 kilometres, or up to around 54 kilometres using rocket-assisted projectile (RAP) ordnance. Of course, this massive range came at a price; higher pressure means that Koksan barrels wear very fast and have an increased risk of getting damaged during firing. Nonetheless, it should be noted that in the early 1970s it made the system by far the longest ranged in existence, with no designs even coming close until decades later. Due to this capacity, the rounds may take minutes to reach their target when fired at the top of their range, allowing for operators to fire a few times and then relocate to avoid destruction.

Two massive M-1978 Koksan SPGs sporting perfunctory camouflage. (KCBC)

M-1978 Koksan SPGs fire their 170mm projectiles during an exercise. Note the separate charges and shells lying on munition boxes in the lower left of the image. (KCBC)

Initial production rates were very low, and the US DoD only became aware of this system by 1978, with three dozen examples known to have been built by the mid 1980s.[12] It is likely production picked up in the late 1980s and since however, and nowadays hundreds of the type and its derivatives are in KPA service. The M-1978 Koksan is known to have been exported in limited numbers to Iran during the Iran-Iraq War of the 1980s where it was used as a long-ranged bunker buster near al-Faw and to bombard Kuwaiti oil fields as punishment for their support of Iraq. At least one example was later captured by Iraqi forces when Iranian positions were overrun and displayed in Iraq after the war. The US intelligence community was initially allowed to transport it to the USA for examination, but upon seeing their eagerness the Iraqis apparently changed their mind, instead allowing unlimited access to it for analysis.[13] The intelligence exploitation team that examined the SPG was reportedly impressed by the design and build quality, as well as the metallurgy (of the barrel, presumably).[14] It was clear Iraqi analysts were themselves clearly intrigued by its capabilities, and it seems Iraq at one point initiated a development programme of its own to create an SPG based on the Koksan and the Soviet 180mm S-23, another extremely long-range towed artillery piece. The result of this programme, a massive 180mm Koksan-inspired SPG based around an East German BLG-60 bridge layer chassis, was later captured by US forces in Iraq's Al Anbar Governorate, near the Anbar university, during a tank removal mission and examined. Nothing else of that programme is known, but it serves as an important reminder of the allure of extremely powerful and long-ranged SPGs such as the Koksan.

Development of the Koksan SPG family continued during the 1970s and early 1980s, spawning at least two different prototypes – both utilising progressively modified chassis – before a new design entered mass production. To increase commonality with the DPRK's growing fleet of Chonma MBTs and to increase support for its massive gun, the second prototype traded the T-55 chassis for a heavily modified Chonma-based chassis, albeit reversed so the weight of the gun was centred where the tank's turret would ordinarily be, as opposed to the engine deck. The final product, given the designator 'M-1989 Koksan' despite being produced since 1983 according to North Korean sources, was further modified with a very thinly armoured cabin at the front and centre of the chassis.[15] This allows for the seating of four crew members and the possible onboard carriage of some munitions, as opposed to the M-1978 Koksan which could not operate without a separate munitions truck. This enables a higher initial fire rate, and its redesigned recoil and firing mechanism likely increases reliability and range to some extent. The new configuration has the additional benefit of being faster to set up, fire and relocate. A new double baffle muzzle brake was also introduced, for what purpose is not entirely clear as both types remain in use today. In its most advanced configuration, the Koksan shows clear resemblance to the Soviet 2S7 Pion, and although it is almost certain the DPRK did not base any aspects of the Koksan directly on this artillery system, it certainly seems to have inspired its ultimate form. It should be mentioned that in line with the current KPA doctrine of virtually never retiring any equipment, the new M-1989 Koksan did not replace the original model, but rather supplemented it, entering service in larger numbers. Although Iran received the older M-1978 Koksan during the Iran-Iraq War, the fact that the M-1989 was also available for export was confirmed by a single example previously in service with the United Arab Emirates Army spotted at an exposition in the United Arab Emirates in 2005. Russia also became a large scale user of the type in late 2024, when it began receiving shipments of artillery from the DPRK to mitigate losses to its long-ranged arsenal incurred by attrition. The choice for the Koksan is notable especially because its unique 170mm calibre is

Iraq's 180mm Koksan derivative being towed by an M88A2 Hercules ARV in 2008. Note the S-23's 'pepper pot' muzzle brake. (United States Marine Corps)

not compatible with Russia stocks. Evidently, the range advantages outweighed logistical considerations. Deliveries progressed surprisingly rapidly, with Ukrainian intelligence claiming as many as 120 had been shipped by January 2025.[16] Meanwhile, South Korea's Joint Chiefs of Staff estimated 220 Koksans and 240mm MRLs had been shipped as of March 2025.[17] While this cannot be verified, footage from Russian railroads suggested at least five separate trainloads had been transferred for a total of 40 or more examples. Since the total number of M-1989 Koksans built is believed to lie in the 150–200 range, it is possible the type is effectively retiring from North Korean service as a result, leaving only smaller numbers of the older M-1978 model.

M-1989 Koksan SPGs during the 105th anniversary of Kim Il Sung's birthday parade of 2017. (NK Pro)

An M-1989 Koksan displayed at the UAE's IDEX 2005. Cut off at the left side of the image, a North Korean 14.5mm Type-64 (a ZPU-4 copy). (Richard Stickland)

Above left: Hundreds of artillery pieces, many of them Koksans firing simultaneously during a massive artillery exercise near Wonsan. (KCBC)

Above right: A triple-barrelled 370mm recoilless gun artillery piece, showcased alongside two M-1989 prototypes and an early Hwasong-5. (KCBC)

Right: A Model 1983 Koksan in Russian service sits in an artillery dugout with a 170mm shell ready to be loaded into its breech. (Unknown author)

North Korean ambitions ran higher than just producing their own SPG variants however, and during the 1980s a large amount of research was invested in finding alternative means to increase the long-range firepower available to the KPA. Attempting to develop an artillery piece with extremely high calibre rivalled only by designs such as the Soviet 406mm 2A3 Kondensator 2P and 420mm 2B1 Oka posed a whole host of novel challenges, many of which had crippled similar high calibre artillery projects. Most importantly, the massive recoil associated with such systems was generally too extreme for components to handle, causing them to wear or break after firing just a few times. Additionally, to prevent overheating and because of the size of individual shells, fire rate attained by massive calibre SPGs is often abysmal. To deal with these issues North Korea chose to take a radically different approach to the problem, and based its prototype on recoilless rifle technology, a unique choice in the field of self-propelled artillery designs. This 370mm monster, based on a Chonma-style chassis – but notably not a reversed one due to the lack of recoil – features three separate barrels to increase its volume of fire, and uses three massive exhaust nozzles to vent gases from the rear, largely eliminating its recoil. Because this design is so different from conventional artillery and since North Korean sources specifically note it as being 'classified', the firing range of the system is very hard to estimate.[18] However, a select handful of historical projects initiated by the Soviet Union and Nazi Germany prior to, during, and shortly after the Second World War examining the feasibility of using oversized recoilless rifles on different platforms shed some light on the possible capabilities of the system. For instance, the Soviet inventor Leonid Vasilyevich Kurchevsky spent most of his research during the early 1930s on developing recoilless rifles of calibres ranging from 37mm to 500mm, based on a multitude of platforms. One of his designs, a 305mm recoilless cannon based on a destroyer named the *Engels*, was constructed and tested in 1934 but ultimately was scrapped due to unsatisfactory results. The weapon, which was outwardly similar to the North Korean 370mm design, was capable of firing a projectile weighing some 330 kilogrammes over a distance of up to 13,500 metres without producing recoil that would stress the destroyer's hull to dangerous extent. However, it was debilitated by an abominable fire rate of roughly one round every hour, caused both by the fact that the propellant and shell had to be loaded separately and that every projectile had to be loaded by crane. Similar problems plagued designs based on the same concept during the early stages of the Cold War, when Soviet engineers attempted to provide the Red Army with a tactical nuclear delivery system in the form of large-calibre self-propelled artillery guns. Due to the range and size demanded by this project one of the prototypes designed to fulfil this role was based on recoilless rifle technology, as the systems responsible for dealing with recoil on such artillery pieces as the 406mm 2A3 Kondensator 2P and 420mm 2B1 Oka were exceedingly complex. The project, which had commenced in 1955, called for the construction of both a 420mm and a 280mm recoilless gun for testing under the designation S-103, the first of which was completed in early 1956. However, after test firing 101 shots both from stationary shooting stands and a tracked chassis the single prototype exploded and was irreparably damaged in late 1956, and the project was shelved before the 280mm variant could even be constructed. In hindsight, the design was considered too complex and inferior to other massive calibre SPGs as well as the ballistic missile designs that swiftly superseded them.

After the 1950s, no other attempts at introducing an artillery piece based on oversized recoilless rifle technology are publicly known until the DPRK took the concept and used it as the basis for their 370mm three-barrelled design, the prototype of which was completed in 1984.[19] Despite being mentioned as part of an exhibition of currently active military equipment, where it was listed as having a crew of five, the system was seen only once in a display of other prototypes, and appears not to have actually entered service. With so little known about the project, the reasons for halting it can only be guessed at. Shortcomings of similar designs such as the ones described earlier appear to have been partially addressed by keeping the system relatively simple, and by installing three separate barrels to increase fire rate and payload. Nonetheless, factors such as a disappointing firing range – possibly comparable to the 13.5 kilometres of Kurchevsky's 305mm design – low accuracy, or unsatisfactory structural integrity might have doomed the ambitious attempt at introducing a wholly novel type of artillery from the start, and it is not impossible the sole example known to exist was merely a mock-up.

New SPG developments after the 1990s were lacking for almost a quarter of a century. Existing designs and production were apparently deemed sufficient to preserve the KPA's artillery advantage over the South even if its technological edge quickly reversed as South Korean artillery pieces such as the K55A1, based on the US M109A2, started entering service. This situation persisted until the 2010s, when a programme possibly spurred on by the introduction and deployment of the ROKA K9 Thunder during the bombardment of Yeonpyeong in 2010 suddenly produced the first new North Korean SPG for decades. Rumbling onto the scene in a surprise unveiling during the parade for the 70th anniversary of the foundation of the DPRK in September 2018, the novel design is an offshoot of the new tank chassis produced at the Kusong tank plant. Based on an enlarged and elongated variant of the chassis also used on the Chonma-216 and Songun-915 which, as on the 1983 Koksan variant, has been reversed, it carries a spacious enclosed turret housing a long 155mm gun, likely L/52. The use of this calibre instead of the conventional 152mm is highly significant as it is typically used by artillery pieces of Western nations, with the notable exception of a number of modern Chinese and Russian export designs. This suggests some relatively recent transfer of SPG technology from either of these nations to the DPRK, although theoretically a wide number of nations operate 155mm artillery. Subtle details in the SPG's design appear to point to the Russian 2S19M1-155 as a likely origin however, which would imply it uses a powerful L/52 gun on a par with almost every other modern SPG design. Notably, it bears much similarity to such SPGs as the K9 Thunder, yet the specifications such as range, fire rate, munition types and perhaps most importantly sophistication of the FCS remain highly speculative. It remains unclear whether the 155mm SPG incorporates an autoloader, but if it does utilise this technology in combination with two-piece munitions this could for instance allow Multiple Rounds Simultaneous Impact (MRSI) tactics. Furthermore, a 2024 visit by Kim Jong Un to the Academy of Defence Sciences gave a glimpse at some of the munitions intended for the new SPG, which included one equipped with what appears to be a close copy of the American M1156 PGK fuse, which converts unguided rounds into GPS-guided ones. The use of this kit, which entered service with Western militaries just a decade ago, would greatly enhance the efficacy of the new SPG by reducing the circular error probable (CEP) of its munitions. Judging by the SPG's exterior and contemporaneous developments, full NBC protection, internal ammunition storage – which was likely lacking in older, more cramped, SPGs – and an advanced FCS seem likely. A dual AGL, dual MANPADS launcher, smoke grenade dischargers and LWR system all seem to be slaved to the latter, aiding it in operations near the volatile front lines, but complicating operations for the crew of five. Examples seen during exercises and later parades omitted the dual MANPADS launcher however, and featured significantly altered turrets, suggesting the design of the SPG was still in flux as development continued. Since the start of the 2020s, a muzzle velocity radar has also been mounted at the base of the gun, further enhancing firing accuracy. The long 155mm gun is likely capable of attaining longer ranges than older SPGs (with the obvious exception of the 170mm Koksan), upwards of 30 kilometres for regular munitions on comparable foreign designs. This once again

Considered too complex and impractical by the only other nation to have actively pursued the development of artillery based on oversized recoilless rifle technology, North Korea nonetheless took the concept and used it as the basis for its 370mm three-barrelled monster before likely reaching the same conclusion as the Soviet Union. The research and development of such a system by the DPRK should be placed in context of its desire to fully exploit any possible technology that might give it an edge over its adversaries, even if these are highly unconventional or considered impractical by other nations. (Artwork by David Bocquelet)

raises the bar for engagement ranges for older South Korean artillery pieces, complicating counter-artillery fire missions and generally threatening ROKA ground operations. The new chassis also offers significant improvements to mobility, and equipment facilitating a deep fording capability was demonstrated. Interestingly, there are some indications suggesting either a dedicated ammunition supply vehicle (similar to the US M992 FAASV) or a command vehicle is also under development. Whether the DPRK is capable of actually mass-producing the new SPG and setting up the required logistics for its novel calibre munitions remains to be seen however, with no more than a few dozen thought to have been produced so far. Furthermore, apparent leakage of hot gases from the bore evacuator during live fire exercises could indicate quality issues in the production of the new SPG's barrel.

North Korea's new 155mm SPG. Note the reversed and modified T-72-derived chassis and extensive weapons package atop the turret. (NK Pro)

The new 155mm SPG during field drills. Note the muzzle velocity radar above the recoil mechanism. (KCBC)

Kim Jong Un inspects a model of the new 155mm SPG in May 2024. Displayed in front are three 155mm munitions, one potentially a RAP variant and another equipped with a copy of the M1156 PGK. In the back, a model of the North's version of the OTO Melara naval gun. (KCBC)

One of the new 155mm SPGs emerges after a test of its fording system, a unique feature for such fighting vehicles. (KCBC)

Multiple Rocket Launchers

Perhaps even more so than in its prolific indigenous SPG projects and experimental weapons designs, North Korea has been industriously engaged in an extremely expansive MRL programme since the start of the 1970s.[20] Having received large batches of Type-63 107mm towed MRLs in the 1960s and BM-21 'Grad' 122mm MRLs later in the same decade, the DPRK swiftly embarked on the task of copying and modifying these systems to suit the North's needs. Although the BM-21 was introduced on the basis of a North Korean Sungri No. 2 truck as early as 1972, it is unclear if the launchers themselves were of indigenous manufacture and it never attained the same degree of popularity in the DPRK as its indigenously designed relative which was designated the 'BM-11' by the US DoD. This domestic MRL, produced since 1973, fires the same 122mm rockets used by the Grad, and has been adapted for use on a variety of platforms. In its original configuration, it is based on the Japanese Isuzu HTW-11, Nissan Diesel TZ50HT, or the Chinese Jiefang CA-30 truck, depending on the production run, with later variants using the externally similar ZiS-151 truck. An easy way to discern the BM-11 and its descendants from the BM-21 is by its launch tubes: all standard BM-11 configurations are equipped with two separate blocks of 3x5 launching tubes, as opposed to a single block of 4x10 tubes of the BM-21, and a redesigned elevation mechanism. The decision to separate the traditionally unified block of launching tubes likely originated in an attempt to increase the maximum effective fire rate and therefore fire density of the system, which stands at roughly four rockets per second, as opposed to the BM-21's two per second. Still more 122mm MRL designs exist within the DPRK, and their ubiquity is showcased particularly well by very simple towed variants with two blocks of 3x3 launch tubes. These are typically towed by tractors during parades, so as to emphasise the fact that even the most basic of civilian assets will be diverted to the war effort in times of conflict.

Right: A North Korean BM-11 122mm MRL based on a ZiS-151 truck. Note the two separate blocks of 3x5 launching tubes. (KCBC)

Below: 122mm MRLs with 2x9 launch tubes towed by tractors during a parade. The use of tractors underlines the fact that civilian equipment (to the extent it can be called such) will be repurposed for military means in the event of war. (KCBC)

Another MRL, the 107mm Type-63, was first copied and produced prolifically in its original towed 3x4 launch tube configuration, sometimes referred to as the Type-75, but the design's versatile nature allowed it to be adapted for many different uses and as such it would later be produced in a variety of sizes on a range of platforms. One example of a mobilised variant of this system produced since 1993 came in the form of a 4x6 or 3x8 block of 107mm launching tubes mounted on an indigenous Sungri-61NA truck equipped with large munition boxes behind the cabin, allowing for the firing of an additional salvo without having to use dedicated resupply vehicles. Since the early 1980s, 323 APC variants were also developed carrying 107mm MRLs for fire support, with more modern variants sporting complete rotating platforms with either 3x6 or 3x8 launch tube blocks for ease of use. In a similar vein, a special variant of the M-1992 APC was developed with a 3x8 launch tube block on its rear. However, it is not clear whether the MRL could be rotated without having to rotate the entire vehicle as well, and its infantry carrying abilities were greatly diminished or even foregone. The contraption has not been seen outside the 1992 parade commemorating the 60th anniversary of the Korean People's Army, and it is unlikely it ever entered service in any significant numbers. While mobile 107mm MRLs abound in KPA service, the towed variant remains by far the most abundant, serving primarily in reserve units for the protection of coastlines or other fortifications. For enhanced effectiveness and versatility, thermobaric, preformed fragmentation and even a cluster warhead with 15 submunitions per rocket were introduced. The latter (amongst regular high fragmentation variants) were even exported to Russia alongside towed 107mm MRLs in 2025, although their effectiveness has not yet been ascertained.[21] There is some evidence that single or dual launchers for infantry use have also been produced.

Above left: Female soldiers position a 107mm MRL in a coastal defence exercise. Although they are hardly suitable in this role, 107mm MRLs are used en masse presumably to counter coastal landings. (KCBC)

Above right: 107mm MRLs on Sungri-61 trucks. While this may seem like just another truck-mounted MRL, this configuration was actually produced in fairly large numbers. Note the box containing additional 107mm rockets behind the cabin. (KCBC)

Left: M-1992 APCs mounting 24-tubed 107mm MRLs during the 1992 parade commemorating the 60th anniversary of the Korean People's Army. (KCBC)

In the meanwhile, the 122mm MRL was installed in a variety of sizes on a whole range of platforms, displaying a gradual increase in professionality of the designs. Earlier variants were relatively simple conversions of Isuzu trucks with two 4x5 blocks of launching tubes, but later variants, one of which (US DoD designation M-1985) based on the indigenously produced Chaju-64 truck, featured a rack for the storage of a salvo of rockets between the cabin and MRL. Interestingly, this line of development progressed throughout the 1980s until a system was created in 1990 (US DoD designation M-1993) that was based on a modified version of the Czechoslovakian 8x8 Tatra T813 truck, which featured a cabin with just two seats and doors instead of the original truck's lengthier cabin. Although the system now seemed heavily inspired by the Czechoslovakian RM-70 MRL of the same calibre, it lacked the cabin armour typically – but not always – fitted and still used the distinctive separated blocks of launching tubes instead of the more common single block of 4x10 tubes. Czechoslovakian influence on the M-1993's design became even more apparent after the parade celebrating the 70th anniversary of the Workers' Party of Korea of 2015, in which it did feature the additional armour on the T813's cabin and was therefore nearly identical to the RM-70 except for the actual MRL and its elevation mechanism. With its second reload at the ready to automatically insert itself into the launch tubes, these MRLs can lay down up to 80 122mm rockets apiece in only a short interval, thus making it one of the more lethal area denial weapons in North Korean service, especially in combination with specialised warheads. These include a thermobaric fragmentation variant that is advertised to attain two to three times the yield of the HE variant, and a cluster variant with 48 submunitions, which has a slightly reduced range of 16 kilometres.[22]

M-1993 122mm MRLs on parade. Note that the launch tubes, as on the BM-11, are separated into two blocks. (KCBC)

Although North Korean development of dedicated 122mm-equipped MRL systems appears to have ended with the M-1993, the widespread export of the BM-11 MRL has led to a wealth of additional variants produced and operated by a myriad of countries across the globe. In fact, the system has ultimately ended up in so many countries that it is often hard to determine whether or not it was originally delivered by the DPRK or by one of the countries that copied it. For instance, after the delivery of BM-11 MRLs to Syria at the start of the 1980s and their subsequent use during the 1982 Lebanon War, several examples were captured by the Israeli military from Syrian-supported militias. After their Syrian career ended in the 90s, the systems were donated to Lebanon where most examples have now ironically been converted to use the ubiquitous

M-1993 122mm MRLs with armoured cabins during the 105th anniversary of Kim Il Sung's birthday parade of 2017. In this configuration, the relation to the Czechoslovakian RM-70 is immediately clear. (NK Pro)

American-made M35 and M809 series trucks as their basis, resulting in a weapons system that is comprised of a Soviet-inspired North Korean-built MRL on a US-made truck.

Perhaps the second most prolific producer of the BM-11 and its derivatives, Egypt, received the system somewhere around the same time as Syria did, and proceeded to produce a multitude of variants based on the original design as the Sakr, with for instance the Sakr-18 referring to the standard 30-tubed system. Countries confirmed to have received Sakr-type MRLs and are still using them include Djibouti, Yemen, Qatar, Ethiopia and Somalia, although it should be mentioned that only Puntland appears to be currently using them in the latter case. Sakr rockets were also delivered to several nations operating the regular Soviet BM-21 MRL, and as such were used during the Syrian Civil War by government forces. Iran, which has set up extensive production lines for several types of BM-11 derived MRLs as well, received its BM-11s slightly after Syria and Egypt and proceeded to make heavy use of them during the Iran-Iraq War. The surviving vehicles continue to be operated alongside indigenous variants of the original design such as the HM-20 to this day. Along with most other nations Libya procured a sizeable batch of BM-11s at the start of the 1980s and gifted an unknown number of these to Sudan after 1989. Some BM-11s in Libya managed to survive until the present day despite receiving little maintenance for decades, a few of which have been converted to use the Brazilian EE-11 Urutu APC as a chassis, and subsequently saw use during the Second Libyan Civil War. Pakistan produces yet another BM-11 derivative as the KRL 122 which typically uses a US M35 truck as its basis, and has exported the type to both Sri Lanka and in recent years Azerbaijan (where it is based on an Ural-4320 truck), which used it during the Second Nagorno-Karabakh War. Other recent Asian recipients of the BM-11 are Myanmar, which also took delivery of other MRLs such as the M-1993, and Bangladesh. Export brochures show custom single or six-barrel 122mm rocket launchers are also offered for export, but because their appearance is unknown and similar systems produced by other nations are ubiquitous, potential customers of those types remain unidentified.

A 122mm BM-11 MRL used by the Army of the Republic of Bosnia and Herzegovina during the Bosnian War. (Authors' archive)

Even though production of various 122mm systems continued well into the 2000s, new variants of its larger calibre successor saw the light of day as early as the mid 1980s. The first 240mm MRL received the designator 'M-1985' by the US DoD, and was built as early as 1984 according to North Korean sources.[23] Employing a calibre that is not commonly used on foreign rocket launchers, except for the much shorter ranged Soviet BM-24, which uses very different munitions, this system consisted of two blocks of 2x3 240mm launch tubes based on Nissan Diesel TZA520 and TZ50HT 6x6 trucks.[24] The 240mm rocket measures 5.2 metres in length, weighs 407 kilograms and packs a warhead of 90 kilograms filled with 45 kilograms of HE.[25] Alternatively, thermobaric, cluster and flechette warheads are known to exist. Its maximum range when used on the 'M-1985' MRL is often reported as being some 43 kilometres, although figures for the maximum effective range are usually estimated at 30 to 35 kilometres by most sources. Nonetheless, existing MRLs used by either side of the Iron Curtain at the time, most notably the Soviet 220mm BM-27 Uragan and US 227mm M270 Multiple Launch Rocket System, had comparable or lower range and warheads with roughly the same weight, making the production of this new system a feat not to be underestimated. Of course, the size increase also has downsides, with specialised reloading equipment required to handle the rockets, whereas 122mm rockets could be loaded by hand.

A system very similar to the 'M-1985', still sporting the same 12-tubed launcher on a more modern Chinese 6x6 Shaanqi SX2150 truck, was conceived in 1985 and received the US DoD designator of 'M-1989'.[26] Even though it is identified as a separate system by the North Korean military itself, it is unknown whether the launcher itself offers any advantages in the areas of range, accuracy and firing speed over the 'M-1985', and despite the fact that the inception of these two systems was separated by no more than a year both were produced in significant numbers, which might imply that the number of suitable trucks available was a greater bottleneck than the ability to produce the launching system.

The 240mm MRL design saw further development during the late 1980s, culminating in the 22-tubed 'M-1991' in 1990. Configured in two blocks of 11 tubes in a pattern of 3x4 with the upper corners left out, this system is likely responsible for unsubstantiated claims that the DPRK also received the 220mm BM-27 Uragan, which has 16 tubes that are arranged in a roughly similar fashion. Possibly because this configuration represented the last major 240mm MRL variant it has been produced on the basis of numerous different trucks, although this might also once again allude to problems faced in acquiring or producing a single homogenous platform to base the launcher on. The variant seen in parades uses an indigenously produced 6x6 truck which is derived from the Chinese Hongyan CQ Series (itself derived from the Romanian ROMAN truck family), but the Hongyan-Steyr 1st Series and in recent times HOWO trucks are used as well. The erecting mechanism was redesigned quite extensively in order to support the larger weight of the launcher, and it is sometimes reported that the range of the system has been increased, although this could also refer to an upgrade performed somewhere during the 2000s which supposedly resulted in a system with a maximum range of 67 kilometres.[27] [28] North Korean sources seem to imply this upgraded variant is considered a new MRL, which has been built since 2011 and has additional modern characteristics such as the capability to use GPS-guided munitions.[29] Yet another, newer variant which began entering service in 2019 utilises armoured Tatra T813-derived trucks, although it remains unclear improvements aside from the launch platform were made. Interestingly, North Korean state media in 2024 alluded repeatedly to the development of new, guided 240mm rockets, tested from a variety of legacy 240mm platforms. Given that GPS-guided rockets had been available for some time for other North Korea MRLs, this might have referred simply to the development of new and more capable variants – although a maximum range of 67 kilometres was apparently retained.[30] [31] The same reports also referred to the development of a new 'automatic fire combined control system' however, suggesting that rather than simply using updated munitions the system's ballistics computer and potentially its integration with

A 240mm 'M-1985' MRL in Iran. This is the most basic 240mm MRL variant produced by the DPRK. (Authors' archive)

A 240mm 'M-1989' MRL in Angola, where the type remains operational to this day. (Forças Armadas Angolanas)

the nation's C4ISR network have been improved as well.[32] They went on to claim that these updates would be rolled out to its 240mm MRL arsenal in the 2024–2026 time frame.[33] The delivery to the armed forces of upwards of 100 240mm MRLs (albeit based on a new lightly armoured 6x6 truck) in May 2024 alone attests that the DPRK's 240mm arsenal is quite formidable indeed, making it one of the types favoured for export to Russia. Yet another variant unveiled as a scale model in 2024, adding to an already incredibly diverse range of platforms associated with the 240mm MRL, seems to draw inspiration from the armoured cab design of the US M142 HIMARS. The continued introduction of new types showcases that the weapons system is not by any means considered obsolete, and in fact constitutes one of the central pillars of the KPA's artillery forces. With its increased range as opposed to older 122mm systems and a fire rate of roughly 33 seconds for its entire 22 round volley, the 240mm family of MRLs is especially dreaded because it could theoretically reach targets well into South Korea and swiftly relocate after firing to avoid retaliation.

A 240mm 22-tube MRL based on a Hongyan-Steyr 1st Series truck during military exercises. (KCBC)

Up-armoured 2019-model 240mm 24-tube MRLs during a delivery ceremony at a stadium in December 2023. (KCBC)

Guided 240mm rockets are launched from a new light chassis in September 2024. Photos of the impacts at a distance of some 60 kilometres suggest a CEP on the order of a few tens of metres or less. (KCBC)

Kim Jong Un tours a display hall at the former Pyeonghwa Motors Factory, where at least 100 new 240mm MRLs were claimed to have been readied for the Western Operational Group in the first half of 2024. (KCBC)

Kim Jong Un inspects a model of a 240mm MRL with an armoured cab that appears to be loosely inspired by that of the US M142 HIMARS during a 2024 visit to the Academy of Defence Sciences. (KCBC)

In addition to being produced in significant quantities for use with the KPA, the 240mm MRL was also exported to at least five different nations, the first of which – Iran – received a large batch of 'M-1985s' in the late 1980s, just in time to still be used in the Iran-Iraq War. This ultimately resulted in the extensive indigenous production of its Iranian derivatives by the designation Fajr-3, which exchange the Japanese Isuzu for German Mercedes-Benz trucks but retain the same 12-barrelled launcher. Angola would later – likely prior to 2000, near the end of the Angolan Civil War – receive the slightly more modern 'M-1989' in unknown quantities, continuing to use them to the present day. Although the UAE received the same systems in the late 1980s alongside other weaponry, the fact that they later moved away from North Korean produced weaponry to more internationally palpable alternatives means they were quickly mothballed. Another operator of the 240mm MRL is Uganda, which still used the larger 'M-1991' variant against ADF/ISCAP forces in DR Congo as of late 2022. Myanmar is also a prolific user of both the 'M-1985' and as recently as 2008 the 'M-1991'. Its 'MAM-02' variant of the 'M-1985' is notably based on new trucks and uses a launch system more reminiscent of the one seen on the 'M-1991', and saw repeated use (and capture) during the Myanmar Civil War. Lastly, Russia took delivery of an unknown number of 240mm MRLs, at least some of which the new-built 6x6 types displayed at Pyeonghwa Motors, from late 2024 onwards for use in the Russo-Ukrainian War.[34]

Most of the scarce funds that would be available over the next two decades, which were marked by the fall of the Soviet Union and subsequent famine (the 'Arduous March'), would be allocated to further development and mass production of 122mm and 240mm systems. Only in the late 2000s another leap in available technology would occur, resulting in tests of a new 300mm system, which has confusingly been referred to as the KN-09, in mid 2014.[35] The MRL itself was finally unveiled during the parade for the 70th anniversary of the founding of the Workers' Party of Korea in October 2015, and although many had anticipated a system based on the Soviet 300mm BM-30, the actual launcher and truck itself appear to have had their roots in China instead. Featuring eight tubes arranged in two blocks of 2x2 barrels based on a modern Chinese 6x6 HOWO truck, the system uses GNSS (global navigation satellite system) guidance to accurately strike targets from a distance as great as 220 kilometres away, putting the entire northern half of South Korea, including its many military bases and airfields, within range. The new MRL's capabilities were underscored when a televised exercise on 3 March 2016, exactly two years after the same drill had been performed, showed at least six missiles being fired from the eastern coast, hitting their targets located on an island some 150 kilometres up coast with negligible CEP. Several modifications to the launch vehicles were apparent during this test, including two square casings around the blocks of launch tubes and blast shields on the windows.[36] The exercise also provided a first good look at the actual missiles employed by the system, which featured a single HE warhead but can presumably be fitted with a range of warheads including thermobaric and cluster munitions. Interestingly, the presence of small fins near the tip of the missile once again shows a similarity to Chinese systems such as the SY300 INS/GPS-guided missile, perhaps suggesting a technology transfer. Successful tests conducted in subsequent months examined the system's abilities out to 220 kilometres, proving it is indeed capable of reaching this impressive range.

Subsequent years would see a more robust roll-out of various types of 300mm MRL platforms. Whereas one example tested in May 2019 used a white civilian truck as its basis, perhaps to demonstrate that these systems could be quite easily concealed during wartime, more recent examples first displayed during the 75th anniversary of the

A KN-09 MRL launches one of its eight massive rockets during tests in 2016. Note the control surfaces on the tip of the rocket. (KCBC)

A 300mm MRL utilising an armoured truck based on the ZIL-135 is inspected by Kim Jong Un during the Self-Defence-2021 exhibition, its guided rocket clearly displayed. (KCBC)

Workers' Party of Korea parade in 2020 constitute a somewhat more professional iteration of the design. Based on a heavy 8x8 armoured truck that is adapted from the 9K52 Luna-M's ZIL-135, it carries two blocks of 2x3 launch tubes, for a total of twelve 300mm rockets. The use of this truck design that is now well over half a century old should be considered suspicious however, and might suggest that instead of indigenously produced these were merely adapted from ZIL-135s that were taken from the Luna-M. Though this makes sense considering the Luna-M's lack of utility (especially compared to the new 300mm MRL), it would mean that these 12-tubed systems are limited both in terms of mobility and the total number that can be produced.

Unconfirmed reports of a classified document distributed amongst senior DPRK officials in early 2017 suggest a large variety of targets had been pre-programmed into these MRL systems, allowing them to quickly strike such targets as the South Korean joint military headquarters in Gyeryong in the initial stages of a war.[37] Supposedly, Kim Jong Un phrased this fact as follows: 'As we have now have a monitoring system and program for multiple rockets, we have completed our preparation to target 10,000 important facilities throughout South Korea. Our goal of reunifying the peninsula has no barrier'. In this capacity, the 300mm MRL must be regarded much more as a strategic weapon than a tactical one, and although it does not appear to fall under the Missile General Bureau command, it performs a role not dissimilar from certain systems that do. Nevertheless, the new MRL is certainly not undefeatable, and its guidance is vulnerable to GPS jamming. Such jammers are likely to be widely employed to defend high value targets during wartime and have the potential of negating the accuracy advantage that makes this weapon so effective almost entirely. This requires proper utilisation of such systems during the chaotic initial stages of a war however, and what inertial guidance that the 300mm missiles are likely to employ may in part make up for this vulnerability.

In a more tactical role, the new MRL could also be highly effective, especially when combined with timely and accurate reconnaissance in order to strike troop concentrations and advancing enemy columns. In this role it could partly compensate for the lack of airpower the KPA is sure to face during a war, providing the equivalent of modern air-launched precision-guided munitions (PGMs) for a low cost. This would require a substantial deployment of the system and the investment of copious resources for its serial production. Still, given that eight or 12 missiles are ready for launch on any given vehicle, relatively few systems are required to allow for an impressive short-term striking capability.

Although the 300mm MRL is the sole new conventional multiple rocket launcher to have entered service since the 1990s, with efforts in the 2000s mainly aimed at introducing more advanced variants of the 122mm and 240mm systems, investments in improving its artillery forces have certainly not ceased in the meantime. Most notable has been the development of new types of shells and rockets, which act as a force multiplier by substantially enhancing each artillery piece's capabilities without requiring the introduction of entire new fighting vehicles. For example, a new guidance section developed for the 122mm rocket used by the majority of its MRL forces allows any 122mm launcher to use GNSS-guided weaponry with a CEP of less than 13 metres.[38] These rockets mostly retain their ordinary range and warhead weight, yet greatly increase the effectiveness of North Korean MRLs by requiring far fewer rockets to accurately strike a specific target. At relatively low cost and effort this has the potential of massively increasing the lethality of the various platforms that use it, especially when combined with proper reconnaissance. Export brochures of the 122mm rockets suggest some severe limitations on their use however, with the guidance section apparently only being effective at ranges between 14 and 19 kilometres.[39] These new technologies are also marketed abroad, and in a deal closed in August 2013 a hundred 122mm rocket control sections were exported to Sudan, which now offers a similar system for export through its Military Industry Corporation (MIC).[40] Interestingly, MIC also markets a range-extended 122mm rocket capable of striking targets up to 40 kilometres away.[41] Although there is no direct proof that these rockets are of North Korean origin, the DPRK does indeed produce an advanced 122mm rocket that is supposedly capable of attaining this range using advances in material and propellant technologies, mirroring developments in many other nations that use this weapon.[42] Combining both developments implies that a massive portion of the KPA's artillery forces now has the potential to outrange virtually all older South Korean artillery pieces with devastating accuracy, depending on the level to which the new missiles are introduced and the effectiveness of counter-artillery detection. Similar research efforts have been undertaken for 240mm MRL systems, which are already known to be using newer rockets with a maximum range of up to 67 kilometres.[43]

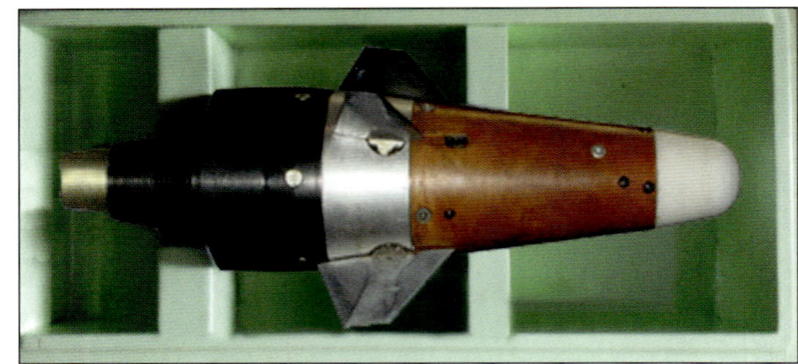

An image showing in intricate detail the GPS-guided variant of a North Korean 122mm rocket fuse. (Wingman Media)

Aside from expanding the mission scope and capabilities of current MRL forces, the introduction of new ammunition is likely to have another side effect beneficial to the KPA. One of the conclusions drawn from analysis of the bombardment of Yeonpyeong in 2010 supposedly yielded that 25 percent of the 122mm rockets impacting the island were duds; an extremely high rate, in effect negating the use of every fourth artillery piece.[44] [45] Newer munitions might well bring more acceptable levels of reliability, and so increase the overall effectiveness of KPA artillery. Nevertheless, both artillery shells and rocket munitions delivered to Russia in late 2023 and early 2024 in support of its invasion of Ukraine evidenced poor storage and packaging practices as well as low manufacturing standards, with mixed reports about their reliability and accuracy as a result. While it is difficult to ascertain the date of manufacture of all munitions delivered given the sheer volume involved (believed to be some 20,000 containers worth of weaponry and 122mm, 130mm, 152mm and 170mm shells, 122mm and 240mm rockets and 60mm, 120mm and 140mm mortars as of mid 2025), the majority examined seemingly stemmed from the 2000–2007 period. For gun artillery it is generally more difficult (though not impossible) to significantly increase ranges simply through the introduction of new artillery rounds, and rounds using GNSS-guidance tend to be prohibitively expensive and unreliable due to the stresses they necessarily endure during firing. Technologies such as Base Bleed and especially Rocket-Assisted Projectiles can and have been used for decades to push the envelope of engagement ranges, but true improvements are likely to require the introduction of entirely new artillery pieces.[46] Since the prospect of large amounts of new types of artillery, for instance utilising autoloaders and modern firing computers to facilitate firing missions such as Multiple Rounds Simultaneous Impact, is currently somewhat implausible – with the new SPG unveiled in 2018 a sole candidate – improvements in gun artillery for the moment will likely remain confined to the continued production of existing artillery types, with modernisation of the MRL forces receiving priority instead.[47]

On the defensive side, the introduction of artillery pieces with better protection and the up-armouring of existing ones represents a simple improvement that currently serves to enhance the survivability particularly of its MRL forces. Primarily of use against shrapnel from nearby explosions, the armour packages appear to have been derived from that of the Czechoslovakian RM-70, with the 240mm 'M-1991' and previously unarmoured 300mm MRLs also currently using their own variants. Continued introduction of new trucks also serves to improve the mobility of newly produced MRLs, allowing for swifter relocation after firing and greater reliability, in turn again enhancing every individual piece's survivability.

There exist further strategies to protect MRL launchers, for instance by preventing the enemy from spotting them. The parade commemorating the 75th anniversary of the founding of the DPRK in September 2023 showcased a small civilian truck and a dump truck that were repurposed to function as MRLs. Such methods not only increase the count of launch platforms available to the KPA during wartime but also renders them exceedingly difficult to detect, as the actual launching mechanism is concealed beneath what resembles a commercial or construction truck. While the presence of these trucks in the parade is not enough to confirm the implementation of this practice on a large scale, the use of concealed launchers might well be anticipated in times of war. Further concealment techniques such as leaving the trucks in their original paint scheme to give the impression of civilian vehicles or implementing mechanisms to conceal the launchers under tarpaulin or plates that move over the launching mechanism on rails when it is not in operation (similar to practices in Iran) can also be adopted for concealment. Nevertheless, each of these practices greatly heighten the likelihood of any truck becoming a target for ROK and US forces during wartime.

Another passive but much more obscure (yet arguably far more important) development concerns the introduction of counter-battery radars. Without these the direction of counter-battery fire is vastly less effective, and many modern militaries including the ROKA invest heavily in these systems as a result. Unfortunately, very little is known on the subject within the DPRK, with identified counter-battery radars dating back to the Cold War-era apparently being based on early-generation Soviet SNAR radars, which were mainly of use against mortars. Nevertheless, it is entirely possible more advanced systems such as the SNAR-10 were also delivered, and in modern times North Korea is known to produce and export unidentified counter-battery radars. One such system was, for instance, included in a deal closed with Mozambique in late 2013 which also concerned a variety of different radars and electronics, indicating extensive investment in these technologies by the DPRK.[48]

With the introduction of more modern MRLs and, to a lesser degree, artillery guns, many older types are freed up from frontline service and can be relegated to other units and reserves. Repurposing old weaponry such as the BM-13, BMD-20 and BM-11 on simple

A 300mm KN-09 MRL on parade, sporting an up-armoured cabin. Note that the square protective covers of the launch tubes seen during tests are not present here. (NK Pro)

towed trailers and relegating them to the Worker-Peasant Red Guard greatly increases the firepower of its reserve forces at no cost, with munitions sourced from old stocks instead of newly produced. Such simple devices and old artillery guns are often towed by artillery tractors and trucks when required, even if of civilian nature, providing the KPA with seemingly endless firepower reserves even if they are by now incredibly outdated. Any nation facing off against the DPRK will surely have to figure out how to combat both its most modern systems as well as the hordes of ancient relics it has managed to maintain, a situation nowadays encountered virtually nowhere else on the planet.

A 132mm rocket is launched by this towed MRL made from a Second World War-era BM-13 Katyusha. (KCBC)

122mm MRLs disguised as commercial trucks seen during a parade held in Pyongyang in 2023. These trucks intend to convey the message that any resource will be dedicated to war should conflict arise. (KCBC)

A 240mm MRL hidden within a dump truck, its true identity concealed under large sacks atop to deceive pilots and drone operators. (KCBC)

3

MILITARY ENGINEERING

With the immense size of the KPA's mechanised units, and with speed being a decisive factor in all stages of the 'One Blow Non-Stop Attack', it is only logical that North Korea has heavily invested in military engineering. Nevertheless, the degree to which it has done so is quite unprecedented, in theory allowing the KPA to overcome most obstacles or difficult terrain that could otherwise slow down or even halt the North's operations during hostilities with the South. On the Korean Peninsula difficult terrain not only consists of rivers and forests, but also of dense urbanised country partitioned by rows upon rows of mountain ranges and valleys. In the inventory of the Korean People's Army Ground Force (KPAGF) this manifests itself through a large force dedicated to military engineering operating a massive inventory of river-crossing equipment, armoured engineering vehicles and other equipment specialised for specific challenges. Aside from crucial infrastructure tasks such as road/bridge repair and facilitating river crossings, military engineering forces are also responsible for the clearing and construction of minefields, ensuring the operability of airfields, constructing fortifications and communication lines and of course recovering damaged vehicles.

Experiences gained in operations during the Korean War gave initial impetus to operating a large military engineering branch, further motivated by the KPAGF's push for mechanisation in the 1970s. Until this time, its development had closely mirrored that of the Soviet Army in equipment, but with strategic thinking increasingly favouring offensive operations as part of any battle, the groundwork for a massive expansion of its engineering branch was laid. Much of its older equipment is therefore Soviet in origin but increasing numbers of indigenous designs of varying sophistication later entered service in far greater numbers, nowadays making up the mainstay of its inventory. Despite the fact that this equipment is specialised for a wide variety of tasks, it is its river-crossing equipment that defines North Korean military engineering above anything else. Possessing close to 1,000 amphibious transports and well over 2,000 pontoon bridging sections, the amount of equipment for river crossing alone already surpasses the inventory of engineering branches of most armies in the world.[1] As with so many branches of the KPAGF, the vast majority of this equipment is of indigenous manufacture. Initially importing K-61, and likely PTS, tracked amphibious transports from the Soviet Union, the DPRK would later commence producing large amounts of indigenous amphibious transports, three main variants of which are nowadays known (designated Sungli, or 'Victory'). The most significant modifications made to the original design were to increase the commonality of components with existing indigenous vehicles such as the 323, thus alleviating stress on its logistics and armament industry. Easily discernible by the number of road wheels (i.e. five and six), the smallest two variants are capable of carrying 29 to 33 passengers and are operated by a single driver. The largest variant, which has seven road wheels, is typically used for hauling vehicles and heavy equipment for which it has a sloped ramp near its rear. As the climate on the Korean Peninsula typically causes rivers to freeze over during winter, especially in the northern half, a special attachment exists to aid in icebreaking and wedging aside readily broken wedges of ice – a truly uniquely North Korean modification. Almost entirely concentrated within the Forward Corps, this force

A five-wheeled amphibious transport with about 30 passengers during a military parade. (KCBC)

A model of a seven-wheeled amphibious transport showcased in the Pyongyang Sci-Tech Complex. This variant is capable of carrying light vehicles. (KCBC)

of nearly a thousand amphibious transports is capable of quickly ferrying personnel and equipment across rivers, allowing infantry to maintain their momentum. Nevertheless, crossing rivers in full gear is still frequently trained by KPAGF infantry for the situations when amphibious transports are not around.

Two Chonma-based armoured bridge layers. Vehicles like these are essential to keeping the military on the move in the river-crossed Korean landscape. (KCBC)

While an impressive portion of North Korean armoured vehicles and transports are amphibious or capable of fording through shallow rivers, allowing for surprisingly fast advances across wet landscapes, important parts of the military still require a different approach. Artillery, mobile air defences, support vehicles and perhaps most importantly logistics generally necessitate bridges or ferries to traverse waters and – given that most regular infrastructure, and particularly those bridges that are of strategic importance, is likely to face swift destruction during war – North Korea has constructed a massive arsenal of pontoon bridging sections. Used to quickly assemble temporary bridges and thus allow larger army units a dry crossing, two major variants are currently in use with the DPRK's military engineering branch. The first requires cranes and heavy manpower to lift individual bridging sections from their trucks one at a time, after which small boats push them into place. The older Soviet TPP pontoon bridge and an indigenous pontoon bridge variant utilise this method, which is time consuming, labour intensive and requires a lot of equipment to set up. The second method, which in North Korea is employed by the Czechoslovakian PMS, uses Soviet PMP-style collapsible bridging sections carried by a Tatra T813 truck which unfold automatically after sliding into the water. This takes up considerably less time, manpower, equipment and additional preparation to carry out. Nevertheless, it is the first indigenous type that is spotted most often, and that seems to make up the mainstay of the KPA's pontoon elements. Aside from pontoon bridges, pontoon ferries such as the Soviet GSP and indigenous variants which require motorboats to push them across bodies of water are also in use. Smaller streams and ditches are dealt with using smaller bridge sections, often carried on trucks and assembled on site by engineers. Aside from this relatively labour intensive and inefficient method, the more conventional (armoured) bridgelayers are also in use, with reported deliveries of Soviet MT-55s, MTU-20s, TMM-3s and East German BLG-60s complemented by at least two indigenous armoured designs based on the Chonma chassis.[2]

Special strategies have been developed for dealing with rivers that have frozen over during winter – a common occurrence especially north of the DMZ. Although infantry and light vehicles may be able to cross on foot, heavier vehicles run the risk of breaking through the ice and sinking, and therefore require a different approach. One

A finished pontoon bridge. Note the heavy manpower required for setting up this bridge type. (KCBC)

A Tatra-813 carrying a PMS pontoon bridge part. These types of pontoon bridges are much faster and easier to set up. (KCBC)

tactic is to simply construct a pontoon bridge on top of the ice, using engineers afoot to put the segments into place, so that any breakings are absorbed by the entire structure and vehicles using it run little risk of falling in. Alternatively, a corridor might be rigged with explosives and so cleared of ice, allowing amphibious vehicles to cross safely and tanks to use their fording equipment. Since chunks of ice still remaining in the free corridor could encumber and damage vehicles using the corridor, which has on occasion been witnessed during exercises, a special vehicle was designed to efficiently scoop up large pieces and shred them. Based on one of the North's indigenous amphibious transports, this equipment is yet another testament to the degree to which the KPA has specialised in operating in the peculiar environment found on the Korean Peninsula.

Aside from engineering vehicles geared towards river-crossing operations, a plethora of other armoured recovery vehicles (ARVs), dozers, trench diggers and mine-clearing vehicles also assist the KPA in a variety of tasks. Soviet-delivered ARVs such as the BTS-2 are once again supplemented by North Korean variants based on the Chonma chassis, sometimes fitted with a 14.5mm KPV for defensive purposes. As production of new tracked chassis continues, new engineering vehicles on that basis are also believed to be introduced, offering more power, reliability and generally improved capabilities. For the design of combat engineering tractors the KPA went with the omnipresent Tokchon chassis, now equipped with a hydraulic dozer blade at the front and a crane on top both patterned after the Soviet BAT-M dozer, which is also in use. These are used mainly for clearing rubble and other obstacles during wartime, thus, for instance, repairing air bases and creating new roads. For the creation of fortifications such machines as the Soviet MDK-2 and BTM are used, although in the DPRK preference often goes out to simply utilising infantry with shovels for this task. However, since vehicles such as the BAT-M, MDK-2, BTM and their indigenous copies are not armoured, they will also be relegated to areas under solid control of the KPA, mainly creating and repairing

A specialised ice clearer based on a six-wheeled amphibious transport during a river-crossing exercise. Note the large blade used for scooping ice onto a receptacle. (KCBC)

The ice is pulverised and then sprayed out to the side of the vehicle, leaving a path safe for amphibious vehicles in its wake. (KCBC)

A BTS-2 ARV on standby during a parade. Should another vehicle break down, it will be used to swiftly remove it. Nevertheless, such occurrences are rare as all vehicles are inspected repeatedly to ensure they will function as required during the parade. (NK Pro)

infrastructure for logistics and units located in the rear. Still more engineering vehicles for use in construction and repairs exist on a variety of different chassis including the Chonma, Tokchon, 323 and many others, though they are often of considerably less sophistication than the aforementioned examples. Additionally, civilian vehicles such as the MAZ-500 series mobile cranes are utilised by the military as well.

A matter perhaps even more pertinent to the KPA than the crossing of rivers or repairing infrastructure is of a rather different nature, however. One of the largest minefields in the world straddles either side of the DMZ and attempting to navigate unprepared through the South Korean end could swiftly stop any invasion dead in its tracks. Different approaches exist to go about clearing such fields, with manually scouring the ground with mine detectors and then dismantling them being the most time consuming to the point where they are mostly of use during peacetime or for mere detection rather than destruction.[3] Many tanks can be outfitted with rollers that set off mines once they go over them, thus clearing a path at relatively minor risk to the vehicle itself; this method appears not to be widely employed by the KPA however, with attachment points for such rigs – or rigs of any kind in fact – usually missing on North Korean-built tanks. An interesting alternative is in using a mine-clearing line charge (MCLC), which is essentially a line charge unfurled by rocket which is set off in order to clear a narrow path of up to 200-metres long through a minefield. In North Korea these systems are based on a 323-chassis (and possibly in a modernised configuration on the

A Tokchon-based CEV. A variety of such vehicles exist, although each type may only have been produced in limited numbers. Soviet variants fill in missing capabilities, making the total picture of North Korean combat engineering capabilities, like most of its military, very complex. (KCBC)

Chunma-D chassis) and will likely be at the forefront of operations should a war break out. Contrarily, the military engineering forces are also responsible for constructing minefields. Although this is typically done by hand, specialised vehicles such as the PMR-3 mechanical minelaying trailer are reported to be in use, and aircraft and MRL systems are also capable of using special munitions to create impromptu minefields.

In exercises military engineering is typically given a fairly high degree of attention, sometimes complicated by the requirement that all operations be conducted under chemical, biological, radiological and nuclear (CBRN) conditions. Given the high likelihood of CBRN weapons usage in a new Korean War, the latter is especially important, and special vehicles and equipment for defence against them abound. Nevertheless, on the whole the military engineering branch is likely due for modernisation. Many of the vehicles and much of the equipment in use stem from the previous century, and in many of the aforementioned niche roles – excepting the river-crossing branch – inventory holdings are believed to be subpar. Since military engineering is absolutely vital to continued effectiveness of the KPA, it is not unlikely that the future will see the introduction of new designs to mend these shortcomings.

Kim Jong Un shares a table with his generals during a visit to Kim Il Sung Military University in 2024. On display are models of a TMM bridgelayer, Chonma-based bridgelayer, Tokchon-based ARV, 323-based mine-clearing line charge, and MAZ-500 crane. (KCBC)

4

MOBILE AIR DEFENCE SYSTEMS

Even if all else succeeds, an advancing army is destined to fail without either aerial superiority or highly capable air defence systems moving alongside. Since the former is for the DPRK an impossibility, it has designed a plethora of self-propelled anti-aircraft guns (SPAAGs) and mobile SAMs in addition to its fixed integrated air defence system (IADS), which will be covered in a separate volume of this series on the Korean People's Army Air and Anti-Air Force (KPAAF). The mobility of these systems means they are harder to detect and, crucially, can advance together into hostile territory, complementing the vast numbers of MANPADS available to the KPA in providing point defence to KPA columns. Boasting a number of impressive indigenous designs, the KPA's mobile air defences have nevertheless lagged behind modern developments for most of the DPRK's history. In recent times, renewed efforts to mobilise its IADS have led to the introduction of several new types of mobile SAMs, once again transforming the threat to opposing air forces.

While practically all air defences of the Korean War and immediate post-war decades consisted of towed anti-aircraft artillery pieces, the DPRK was not a total stranger to the SPAAG concept. Indeed, even during the first parade of the KPA on 8 February 1948 several GAZ-AA trucks with 12.7mm DShKs mounted on their rear were showcased. Other early mobile AA is believed to have included 14.5mm ZPUs installed on train wagons for protection of important deliveries of supplies. Nevertheless, it was only once the mechanisation of the 1970s got going in earnest that the DPRK began to look for mobile AA systems to support its newly established offensive capabilities. Instead of importing SPAAGs from abroad like so many Soviet-influenced countries did during the Cold War, the DPRK once again decided to rely on indigenous production of systems to suit their needs. Unsurprisingly, the ubiquitous 14.5mm ZPU-4 serves as the basis for many of these systems, often consisting of the simple mating of the system to several types of trucks, sometimes further supported by MANPADS on simple mounts.[1] More advanced systems utilise the 323 APC chassis for mounting the ZPU-4, an up-armoured variant of which is designated the M-1983 by the US DoD. Although these vehicles are plentiful in the KPA, the fact that they are manually aimed, unguided and feature an unimpressive calibre for AA purposes means they are of little use against anything but helicopters on the modern battlefield. A more advanced intermediate design came in the form of the 'M-1978', which combines the Chinese 37mm Type 65 dual AA gun with a Tokchon chassis. In effect, it bears a resemblance to the US M19 Multiple Gun Motor Carriage, several of which were captured from US forces in the Korean War and by which design it might well be inspired. Although its cyclic rate of fire is higher, the M-1978 is similarly hampered by the lack of any radar guidance or even an automatic feeding system, severely limiting its capabilities. The three-man gun crew (for a total of five for the entire vehicle) has to deal with a very cramped open turret, which in addition to the gun system sometimes also includes a dual MANPADS mount. Its unimpressive capabilities led to it being produced only sparingly, with only a limited number deployed by the mid 1980s when production shifted to its successor.[2]

Although it is sometimes reported that the KPA also operates the ZSU-57-2, or alternatively that some 250 ZSU-57-2 turrets were mounted on Type-59 chassis imported from China, there is no evidence the DPRK actually received or operated the system.

However, a SPAAG very closely resembling the ZSU-57-2 has been produced indigenously and has been given the designation 'M-1985' by the US DoD. Based on the North Korean variant of the 57mm S-68A fitted in a turret on a chassis closely resembling the Soviet GM-575 – also used as a basis for the ZSU-23-4 – it inherits the drawbacks of the S-68A, including its hand-fed five round clips, yet constitutes a potent threat. Although it was designed as an AA gun, this system would also be especially useful against ground targets due to its high rate of (burst) fire and the powerful fragmentation damage dealt by the 57x348mmSR round. Since it is not radar-guided, its targets remain limited to those in visual line of sight – yet experiments with radar-guided SPAAGs commenced in the early 1980s as well. By far the most capable SPAAG publicly confirmed to be in service, and the only one that is radar-guided, it was supposedly designated the M-1989 (and later M-1992) by the US DoD, even though declassified CIA documents reveal that a prototype of the system was first spotted in late 1983.[3] It is believed small numbers of ZSU-23-4s were delivered at the start of the 1970s, and it is clear this is where the M-1989 has its roots. Using the same chassis as the M-1985, it features the AK-230 dual 30mm naval cannon as its main armament, and is directed by a radar very reminiscent of the Shilka's RPK-2 'Tobol', although it is more likely to be based on the MR-104 'Drum Tilt' radar with which the DPRK was experimenting at the time. Despite the fact that its fire rate is almost half that of the ZSU-23-4 at a cyclic rate of some 2,000 rounds per minute, the 30x210mmB round has a higher muzzle velocity and packs a much greater punch, resulting in a performance that is likely to be comparable to the Shilka at short range, but effective out to a longer distance.

Several GAZ-AA trucks armed with 12.7mm DShK heavy machine guns seen during the first parade of the KPA in 1948. (KCBC)

37mm SPAAGs on parade; note that two MANPADS can be fitted to the rear of the vehicle. This early SPAAG variant is nowadays only seen rarely. (KCBC)

In the 1990s, this SPAAG was succeeded by a newer design based around the same chassis but sporting the 30mm six-barrelled rotary cannon derived from the AK-630 that had recently been developed. Using the slightly slower but generally more efficient 30x165mm round, it supports a firing rate of 5,000 rounds per minute and has an effective firing range of up to four kilometres. Additionally, four MANPADS are mounted in boxes beside the turret, providing a SAM capability within the same engagement ranges to enhance its short-range air-defence (SHORAD) efficacy. For guidance, it utilises a separate target tracking radar and a longer-ranged target acquisition radar, both of which were newly developed. Although no images of this air-defence system in KPA service are available, it was pictured in a North Korean arms brochure marketed to an African country and is believed to have received the US DoD designation

57mm SPAAGs during the 100th anniversary of Kim Il Sung's birthday parade in 2012. Vehicles such as these remain useful in the ground support role, yet the North Korean variant appears to be unable to train its cannons on ground targets. (David Flack)

A rare image of a North Korean ZSU-23-4 'Shilka' next to an indigenous 30mm SPAAG. (KCBC)

of 'M-1994'. The exceedingly high cyclic fire rate of this system combined with the option of complementing it with MANPADS makes it a very effective short-ranged threat, although it remains to be seen in what numbers it was produced. Nevertheless, it certainly constitutes the most capable short-ranged air-defence system in use with the KPA, likely serving with elite frontline units in order to provide protection from opposing close air support aircraft and helicopters for advancing columns.

Indigenous 30mm SPAAGs during the 100th anniversary of Kim Il Sung's birthday parade in 2012. (David Flack)

Further indigenous projects consist of the relatively simple mating of MANPADS to vehicles modified for this purpose. At least two variants exist, the first of which consists of the addition of a simple superstructure on a 323 APC for the mounting of four MANPADS, replacing the characteristic turret mounting two 14.5mm KPVs. The second uses the M-1992 APC as its basis, with a modified aft on which an automated quadruple MANPADS mount has been placed. This vehicle has only been spotted in the KPA Exhibition of Arms and Equipment and might not actually be in use with the KPA in any significant numbers.

Aside from these indigenous short-ranged systems, the only mobile SAM system tasked with providing point defence in service is the Soviet-legacy Strela-10M, delivered to the KPA together with BTR-60PU-12 air defence command vehicles during the 1980s and designated the Pongae-3 despite never entering indigenous production. The effectiveness of this system is somewhat dependent on the type of missiles employed, as the Strela-10 can fire a range of different variants with varying specifications. This flexibility was shown to have been fully exploited by North Korea during the parade for the 105th anniversary of Kim Il Sung's birthday in 2017, when the system was driven through the streets of Pyongyang fitted with two canisters each carrying four of the DPRK's Igla-derived MANPADS.[4] Nonetheless, despite the advantages the Strela-10 offers over its simpler alternatives in the form of MANPADS-derived systems, its range remains similarly limited to under five kilometres. Perhaps the greatest shortcoming in the KPA's equipment is therefore not unsurprisingly a mobile medium-ranged air defence system to mend the gap between point defence systems such as the Strela-10M and fixed strategic systems such as the S-75. Despite efforts to ameliorate this issue by modifying existing SAMs to suit this purpose

A North Korean Strela-10 carrying two boxes with four MANPADS each instead of its usual loadout during the 105th anniversary of Kim Il Sung's birthday parade of 2017. (NK Pro)

the problem persists, and as it stands there is little reason to believe a modern opposing force would have especially much difficulty neutralising the North Korean IADS during a new Korean War. While some systems that might be capable of (partially) filling the gap were paraded in the early 2020s, these have yet to be demonstrated during publicised tests and thus remain an unknown factor.

The most widely deployed SAM modification thus far mirrors developments in a variety of ex-Soviet and/or client states, mating the S-125's launcher to a mobile platform to create a relatively capable self-propelled medium-ranged SAM system. Partially addressing a dire shortcoming in the North Korean IADS in this manner, the DPRK is only the latest country to mobilise the S-125 since Russia, Poland and Iraq started producing similar systems during the early 2000s, with Iraq deploying it operationally against coalition air forces in 2003. Many more countries now have mobile S-125s in service, yet the North Korean version should not be underestimated; both in its own right and as a representation of a wider ongoing mobilisation of its air defence forces the new system signifies a worrying development. Although the North Korean version was only displayed during the parade for the 100th anniversary of Kim Il Sung's birthday in 2012, images of Kim Jong Il inspecting a variant based on a towed trailer suggest the DPRK was already experimenting with increasing the mobility of its S-125 and S-75 static SAMs before the end of 2011. Although it should have been possible for North Korea to set up production lines for most parts of the launch vehicle and missiles, it appears at least some were in fact imported from Cuba to keep costs down. These launchers were crudely cut into pieces in order to fit in the shipping containers, leading inspectors to wonder about the apparent carelessness with which these weapons systems were transported. In fact, the damage was actually indicative of their eventual destination: those parts that were cut off would not be required on the North's mobile S-125. Nevertheless, if all launchers are cannibalised from existing imported systems this would severely limit the degree to which the new SAM can be introduced into the KPA. The quadruple 5P73 launchers were used to create the dual launch rails for the mobile system, with the regular radar suite of SNR-125 'Low Blow', P-15 'Flat Face A' and PRV-11 'Side Net' radars apparently towed to launch sites. Interestingly, the cargo ship *Chong Chon Gang* which was seized in Panama in July 2013 carried not only launchers and missiles for this system, as well as the S-75, but also what appears to be a single Cuban phased array antenna for the P-19 'Flat Face B'.[5] While this cargo shipment of course did not arrive at its destination, it is likely that earlier shipments did, and that this system is now in limited use for aiding North Korea's mobile S-125s. The mere mobilisation of this SAM is therefore likely not the full extent of upgrades, and radar suite and command module modernisations are to be expected. Although the launcher has so far only been seen operationally mounted on the Soviet KrAZ-255B truck, a prototype based on the more modern Belarusian MAZ-630308-224 also exists. Experience maintaining, refurbishing and improving the S-125 was also put to commercial use, with both Tanzania and Mozambique reportedly contracting North Korean companies to repair and upgrade their S-125 SAMs and associated systems in the early to mid 2010s.[6]

One of four Cuban S-75 launchers destined for North Korea discovered onboard the *Chong Chon Gang*. (UN Panel of Experts)

One of two S-125 launchers found aboard the *Chong Chon Gang*. Note the crude cuts made in order to fit the launcher into its container – the fact that these parts were not needed for the mobile S-125 conversion is likely to have driven this decision rather than mere carelessness. (UN Panel of Experts)

A mobile S-125 on a KrAZ-255B truck launching its missile during an exercise in 2015. (KCBC)

Another image showing the mobile S-125's dual launcher in more detail. (KCBC)

Even though the S-125's two-staged solid fuel V-601 missiles, which do not appear to have been upgraded for the mobile variant, are much more manoeuvrable and are therefore more likely to hit a modern target, they are quite limited in range in comparison to, for instance, the S-75. Likely for this reason another programme was initiated for the development of a mobile S-75 based on a Taepaeksan-96 truck. The idea for this conversion may well have come from Cuba, which bases its mobile S-75s on the T-55's chassis. However, the North Korean design combines this mobility upgrade with a modified V-750 missile which houses an IR sensor in its nose cone, rendering it much more electronic countermeasure (ECM) resistant by using its IR seeker head to find the target in the last stage instead of relying on the sensitive radar suite. It also allows the radar system to shut off after targeting, rendering the radar less susceptible to suppression of enemy air defences (SEAD). This was likely done using the IR seeker of the R-24T air-to-air missile of the KPAAF's MiG-23MLs, mirroring efforts made by the Iraqis to perform a similar conversion to their 3M9 missiles of the 2K12 SAM system. Since radar systems are likely to endure heavy jamming and SEAD practices during war, this ensures the missiles will retain at least some chance of hitting their intended targets. The mobile S-75 has yet to be seen deployed in the field, but even if its production remains limited the widespread introduction of IR seeker-equipped missiles amongst existing S-75 sites could constitute a significant increase in their capabilities. Especially combined with the upgrades in the command module which are expected to have taken place, a variety of new tactics could be used to maintain the relevance of this veritably ancient SAM design, which had its first combat test in late 1959. Nevertheless, its age shines through in its dangerous hypergolic liquid propellants and poor manoeuvrability, and advances in seeker and guidance technology or new Transporter Erector Launchers do not conceal the need for truly modern mobile air defences. In particular, despite the stopgap measures of mobilising fixed Soviet-legacy SAMs, a dedicated medium-ranged self-propelled SAM is sorely lacking in the DPRK's IADS. Between MANPADS and SPAAGs and more strategic systems such as the Pongae-5 and other new systems (which are also mobile, but fall under KPAAF command and require considerably more time to set up), a SAM system such as the Soviet 9K37 Buk would be highly desirable, and is a likely candidate for future developments. And indeed, the 90th anniversary of the Korean People's Revolutionary Army in April 2022 showcased for the first time a heavy tracked system that might fall into this category. Based on a heavily armoured Songun-915-derived chassis with seven road wheels, it carries eight large missile canisters whose use is currently unknown save for the fact that the vehicle featured in the air defence section of the parade. A more complete examination of systems in this class, which are thought to fall under KPAAF command, is included in the relevant volume of this series.

Kim Jong Il inspecting an S-75 fitted with an IR seeker. The widespread introduction of such missiles in existing SAM sites may significantly increase the threat posed by this archaic system. (KCBC)]

Despite having been designed in the early 1990s, it is believed that the 'M-1994' is the most modern SPAAG to have been produced by the DPRK thus far. Like many other promising arms projects, it remains to be seen if the DPRK has directed the required funds for the acquisition of enough vehicles to provide a sufficient SHORAD capability for its troops. The vehicle is seen here with the MANPADS boxes beside the turret and its target tracking radar (front) and target acquisition radar (rear) deployed. (Artwork by David Bocquelet)

Mating the S-125's launcher to a mobile platform creates a relatively capable self-propelled SAM system at low cost. As with the self-propelled S-75 SAM system, the acquisition of launchers and missiles from Cuba allowed the DPRK to assemble several systems without the need to disband any of its current static SAM sites. However, as a consequence the number of self-propelled launchers is unlikely to surpass more than a handful, at least until the DPRK begins using its own launchers for conversion as well. The system is seen in its prototype configuration based on the Belarusian MAZ-630308-224 truck. (Artwork by David Bocquelet)

Combining the mobility of the MAZ-630308-224 truck with an IR seeker-equipped V-750 missile created what was at the time of its introduction a quite potent SAM. With a static SAM network that struggles to maintain its relevance in the era of cruise missiles and SEAD, the conversion of more S-75s is a cost-efficient method at providing some deterrent to ROK and US airpower. (Artwork by David Bocquelet)

BIBLIOGRAPHY

Berger, Andrea. *Target Markets* (Abingdon: Routledge, 2015)

Bermudez Jr., Joseph S. *Shield of the Great Leader: The Armed Forces of North Korea* (St Leonards: Allen & Unwin, 2001)

Federal Research Division. *North Korea a country study* (Washington, DC.: Federal Research Division, 2008)

Gerardi, Greg J,. James A. Plotts. *An Annotated Chronology of DPRK Missile Trade and Developments* (Monterey: Nonproliferation Studies at the Monterey Institute of International Studies, 1994)

James Martin Center for Nonproliferation Studies at the Monterey Institute of International Studies *North Korea Missile Chronology* (Washington, DC.: Nuclear Threat Initiative, 2012)

Kim Il Sung, *The present situation and the tasks of our party; report at the conference of the Workers' Party of Korea* (Pyongyang: Foreign Languages Pub, 1966)

Korean Overseas Information Service. *Undermining Peace: North Korea's Infiltration Tunnels* (Seoul: Korean Overseas Information Service, 1991)

Marine Corps Intelligence Activity. *North Korea Country Handbook* (Quantico: Marine Corps Intelligence Activity, 1997)

Ministry of National Defence of the Republic of Korea. *Defense White Papers 2006-2018* (Yongsan, Seoul: Ministry of National Defence of the Republic of Korea, 2006-2018)

Sang-Hoon Chung, Joseph. *North Korea's "Seven Year Plan" (1961-70): Economic Performance and Reforms in Asian Survey Vol. 12 No. 6* (Berkeley: University of California Press, 1972)

Singlaub, John K. et al. *Hazardous Duty* (New York City: Touchstone, 1992)

Ustyantsev S. Kolmakov D. *T-72/T-90 Experience in developing domestic main battle tanks* (Nizhny Tagil: UVZ, 2013)

ENDNOTES

Chapter 1

1 Information obtained from the KPA Exhibition of Arms and Equipment in Pyongyang.

2 Central Intelligence Agency. 'Trends in North Korea's Ground Forces' (1986) *CIA FOIA* https://www.cia.gov/readingroom/document/cia-rdp88t00539r000400490002-2

3 Nevertheless, the US DoD assessed at the time that the Soviets were cooperating with this project. Both this possibility and that of a self-supported project remain open.

4 Referring to a legendary flying horse that is of importance in North Korean mythology.

5 Central Intelligence Agency. 'Trends in North Korea's Ground Forces' (1986) *CIA FOIA* https://www.cia.gov/readingroom/document/cia-rdp88t00539r000400490002-2

6 Joost Oliemans, Stijn Mitzer 'North Korea and Ethiopia, brothers in arms' (2014) *NK News* https://www.nknews.org/2014/09/north-korean-military-support-for-ethiopia/

7 Of course, to much of the Soviet-aligned world a far more capable alternative soon became available in the form of the T-72.

8 Information obtained from the KPA Exhibition of Arms and Equipment in Pyongyang.

9 Fording is a process wherein the tank is made airtight and a snorkel tube is attached to the turret so that air can be circulated while the tank drives across the riverbed. Soviet tanks and their North Korean derivatives are as a rule capable of fording through waters up to five metres deep. Tellingly, while US armour often cannot ford, the South's indigenous designs such as the K1 and K2 can, albeit requiring logistics vehicles to supply the snorkels (which are wide enough to allow crew evacuation in an emergency, unlike the North's snorkels).

10 Central Intelligence Agency. 'Trends in North Korea's Ground Forces' (1986) *CIA FOIA* https://www.cia.gov/readingroom/document/cia-rdp88t00539r000400490002-2

11 Ustyantsev S. Kolmakov D. T-72 / T-90 Experience in developing domestic main battle tanks. (Nizhny Tagil: UVZ, 2013)

12 Likely referring to the T-72M1.

13 The Soviet Union generally stuck to producing tanks with cast turrets, finding their homogeneity and precise shape to provide sufficient advantage to warrant the difficult production process. Like the West and North Korea in the 1990s, it would switch to welded turrets with the advent of the T-90A.

14 Information obtained from the KPA Exhibition of Arms and Equipment in Pyongyang.

15 The Juche year count, which started at Juche 1 with the birth of Kim Il Sung in 1912.

16 Munhwa Broadcasting Corporation. '체포된 북한 스파이 소지 러시아제 기관총,특수무기[박영민]' (1995) *MBC News* https://imnews.imbc.com/replay/1995/nwdesk/article/1964742_30705.html

17 Information obtained from the KPA Exhibition of Arms and Equipment in Pyongyang.

18 Information obtained from the KPA Exhibition of Arms and Equipment in Pyongyang.

19 Information obtained from the KPA Exhibition of Arms and Equipment in Pyongyang.

20 It should be mentioned that such a description of armour means fairly little, as armour values are usually compared in terms of Rolled Homogeneous Armour (RHA) equivalent against specific types of projectiles. Taking some liberty however, one could interpret this to mean the Songun-915's frontal turret armour has an effective (i.e. taking armour angles into account) RHA equivalency of 900mm against HEAT projectiles – which is comparable to the armour protection values of the T-90.

21 Information obtained from the KPA Exhibition of Arms and Equipment in Pyongyang.

22 Information obtained from the KPA Exhibition of Arms and Equipment in Pyongyang.

23 Information obtained from the KPA Exhibition of Arms and Equipment in Pyongyang.

24 Information obtained from the KPA Exhibition of Arms and Equipment in Pyongyang.

25 Blowout panels are designed to fracture in the event of an explosion, thus directing ignited propellants and fumes away from the crew compartment.

26 There was also however reason to suggest not all of these were fitted with the requisite electronics and optics, with possibly just a select few being fully functional as a result.

Chapter 2

1 In which multiple batteries time the arrival of their rounds for maximum impact.

2 One particularly poignant example of this is the 1960s era 2K6 Luna artillery rocket serving alongside the newest 300mm MRL. The latter is precision-guided with a negligible CEP (circular error probable), eight missiles per carrier, and a range of well over 200 kilometres, whereas the former carries a single rocket with a CEP

of some 800 metres and a range of 45 kilometres. The difference in warhead weight does little to offset the 300mm MRL's advantage over the 2K6, and yet both systems continue to see service.

3 Information obtained from the KPA Exhibition of Arms and Equipment in Pyongyang.

4 Information obtained from the KPA Exhibition of Arms and Equipment in Pyongyang.

5 Information obtained from the KPA Exhibition of Arms and Equipment in Pyongyang.

6 Information obtained from the KPA Exhibition of Arms and Equipment in Pyongyang.

7 This SPG is also affectionately nicknamed the 'rubber duck' for its peculiar looks by the authors.

8 Not to be confused with the Koksan, which is confirmed to be designated Juche Po ('Juche gun') in the DPRK. The actual name of the second SPG line is unknown, and it is possible that Juche Po was only attributed to it by mistake.

9 Information obtained from the KPA Exhibition of Arms and Equipment in Pyongyang.

10 Central Intelligence Agency. 'North-South Korea: The Artillery Race' (1987) *CIA FOIA* https://www.cia.gov/readingroom/document/cia-rdp88t00539r000600800002-5

11 South Korean artillery pieces fell vastly short of the ranges of most of what North Korean artillery had to offer even before the introduction of the Koksan. Only the handful of 175mm M107 SPGs and the 155mm KH-179 towed howitzer entering service since 1984 could retaliate against weapons such as the 130mm M-46 field gun and its North Korean derivatives.

12 Central Intelligence Agency. 'North-South Korea: The Artillery Race' (1987) *CIA FOIA* https://www.cia.gov/readingroom/document/cia-rdp88t00539r000600800002-5

13 Rick Francona. 'North Korean M1978 Koksan Gun – the Iranian angle' (2017) *Middle East Perspectives* http://francona.blogspot.com/2017/08/north-korean-m1978-koksan-gun-iranian.html

14 Rick Francona. 'The Awakening - IAEA and the real "axis of evil"' (2009) *Middle East Perspectives* http://francona.blogspot.com/2009/06/iaea-tells-us-what-have-known-for-some.html

15 Information obtained from the KPA Exhibition of Arms and Equipment in Pyongyang.

16 Martin Fornusek. 'North Korea to send artillery units, 150 more ballistic missiles to aid Russia's war, Budanov says' (2025) The Kyiv Independent https://kyivindependent.com/north-korea-to-send-artillery-units-150-ballistic-missiles-to-aid-russias-war-budanov-says/

17 Lee Minji. '(LEAD) N. Korea presumed to send at least 3,000 more troops to Russia: JCS' (2025) *Yonhap News Agency* https://en.yna.co.kr/view/AEN20250327002251315

18 Martin Fornusek. 'North Korea to send artillery units, 150 more ballistic missiles to aid Russia's war, Budanov says' (2025) The Kyiv Independent https://kyivindependent.com/north-korea-to-send-artillery-units-150-ballistic-missiles-to-aid-russias-war-budanov-says/

19 Martin Fornusek. 'North Korea to send artillery units, 150 more ballistic missiles to aid Russia's war, Budanov says' (2025) The Kyiv Independent https://kyivindependent.com/north-korea-to-send-artillery-units-150-ballistic-missiles-to-aid-russias-war-budanov-says/

20 Though it remains unconfirmed, there are reasons to suggest the 200mm BMD-20 was indigenously produced prior to the 1970s.

21 Mads Brügger. *The Mole: Undercover in North Korea.*

22 Mads Brügger. *The Mole: Undercover in North Korea.*

23 Plaque displayed during 2024 visit to Academy of Defence Sciences.

24 Another 240mm MRL that saw the light of day in 1984 according to North Korean sources supposedly sported 18 barrels. However, since this configuration has never been identified in available footage nor been described by the US DoD or any other sources, it is unknown what its specifics are, or even whether or not it actually ever had a significant production run.

25 Information obtained from the KPA Exhibition of Arms and Equipment in Pyongyang.

26 This truck is also used by the PLA to carry a 40-tubed Type-81 122mm MRL system.

27 Yonhap News Agency '(4th LD) N. Korea fires 25 short-range missiles toward East Sea' (2014) *Yonhap News Agency* https://en.yna.co.kr/view/AEN20140316003053315

28 박영자. '김정은 정권의 대남 긴장조성: 2013 년과 향후 전망' Korea Institute for National Unification

29 Information obtained from the KPA Exhibition of Arms and Equipment in Pyongyang.

30 Kim Soo-yeon. 'N. Korea says it newly developed shells for multiple rocket launcher' (2024) *Yonhap News Agency* https://en.yna.co.kr/view/AEN20240212000800315

31 KCNA. 'DPRK Academy of Defence Sciences Conducts Test-fire of 240 mm-caliber Controllable Multiple Rocket Launcher Shells' (2024) KCNA Watch https://kcnawatch.org/newstream/1728521201-221889360/dprk-academy-of-defence-sciences-conducts-test-fire-of-240-mm-caliber-controllable-multiple-rocket-launcher-shells/

32 Glocom markets such networking solutions under the name 'GS-2210 Artillery Fire Control System'.

33 'Respected Comrade Kim Jong Un Oversees Test-Fire of Controllable Shells for Multiple Rocket Launcher' (2024) *Minju Joson Offices of the DPRK*

34 Ukrainian intelligence suggested as many as 120 had been delivered by January 2025, but evidence supporting such extensive transfers has yet to emerge.

35 The same designation was at the time used, apparently incorrectly, for a new anti-ship missile system.

36 But interestingly, not on most examples seen during parades and exercises hence.

37 Jeong Yong-Soo, Kang Jin-Kyu. 'Document says North now has guided 300mm launchers' (2017) *Korea JoongAng Daily* http://koreajoongangdaily.joins.com/news/article/article.aspx?aid=3034911

38 United Nations Security Council. 'Report of the Panel of Experts established pursuant to resolution 1874 (2009)' 27 February 2017 *UNSC*

39 Mads Brügger. *The Mole: Undercover in North Korea.*

40 Information obtained from Sudan's Military Industry Corporation http://mic.sd/en/home/products/

41 Information obtained from Sudan's Military Industry Corporation http://mic.sd/en/home/products/

42 Yonhap News Agency. '(LEAD) N. Korea deploys 300 new MLRS along front line: sources' (2016) *Yonhap News Agency* https://en.yna.co.kr/view/AEN20160424001100315

43 Yonhap News Agency. '(LEAD) N. Korea deploys 300 new MLRS along front line: sources' (2016) *Yonhap News Agency* https://en.yna.co.kr/view/AEN20160424001100315

44 It should be noted that if correct, this figure still includes some rounds fired by 76.2mm coastal artillery guns. These are presumably of the exceedingly old ZiS-3 type, which was developed during the Second World War and likely uses rounds that have lain in stock for many decades.

45 Joseph S Bermudez Jr. 'The Yŏn-p'yŏng-do Incident, November 23, 2010' (2011) *38 North* https://www.38north.org/wp-content/uploads/2011/01/38North_SR11-1_Bermudez_Yeonpyeong-do.pdf

46 Base Bleed is a technique whereby a small gas generator is used to diminish drag behind an artillery round and thus increase range by a certain percentage at the cost of some accuracy. Rocket-Assisted Projectiles instead use an actual rocket motor embedded in the round which engages during flight to significantly boost range mainly at the cost of complexity. The second is confirmed to be in use for a variety of North Korean calibres.

47 In this firing mode multiple rounds are fired in succession by the same gun using different propellant chargers and different trajectories, resulting in all rounds landing on the target at the same time for maximum impact.

48 United Nations Security Council. 'Report of the Panel of Experts established pursuant to resolution 1874 (2009)' 27 February 2017 *UNSC*

Chapter 3

1 Republic of Korea Ministry of National Defense. 'Defense White Papers 2006-2022' *ROK MoD*

2 Marine Corps Intelligence Activity. 'North Korea Country Handbook' (1997) *DoDIPP*

3 Since North Korea is still covered with unexploded ordnance (UXO) dropped during the Korean War, even during peacetime

explosive ordnance disposal teams are active and even trained by the Red Cross.

Chapter 4

1 The domestic version of the ZPU-4 (known as the Type-64) was also exported prolifically, including to the UAE and Malta.
2 Central Intelligence Agency. 'Possible Production Of New Air Defense Weapon System' (1983) *CIA FOIA* https://www.cia.gov/readingroom/document/cia-rdp91t00712r000200510005-1
3 Central Intelligence Agency. 'Possible Production Of New Air Defense Weapon System' (1983) *CIA FOIA* https://www.cia.gov/readingroom/document/cia-rdp91t00712r000200510005-1
4 Such a conversion is not entirely unprecedented, as Russian Strela-10s also have the option of using the Strelets quadruple Igla mount instead of their usual missiles. In general, modern MANPADS offer comparable performance to most types of missiles traditionally used by the Strela-10, and as such replacing them is a natural course of action. Though the Strela-10M is reportedly known as the Pongae-3 in North Korea, the MANPADS-equipped variant is apparently referred to as the Hwaseong-Chong ('Arquebus'), same as the MANPADS.
5 United Nations Security Council. 'Report of the Panel of Experts established pursuant to resolution 1874 (2009)' 6 March 2014 *UNSC*
6 United Nations Security Council. 'Midterm report of the Panel of Experts submitted pursuant to resolution 2345 (2017)' 5 September 2017 *UNSC*

ABOUT THE AUTHORS

Joost Oliemans is an analyst and author focusing on Asia, the Middle East and North Africa. Together with Stijn Mitzer, he is the author of *The Armed Forces of North Korea: On the Path of Songun*. Joost Oliemans also writes for various news agencies and websites about military-related matters.